Artificial Intelligence For Quantum Machine Learning

Exploring the Intersection of Quantum Computing and AI

Hedwig Garrett

Table of Contents

Artificial Intelligence For Quantum Machine Learning: Exploring the Intersection of Quantum Computing and AI

PART II: QUANTUM MACHINE LEARNING CONCEPTS

Chapter 4: What is Quantum Machine Learning (QML)?

- The Intersection of AI and Quantum Computing
- Key Differences Between Classical ML and Quantum ML
- Potential Benefits and Challenges of QML
- **Flowchart:** How Quantum Machine Learning Works

Chapter 5: Quantum Data Representation in AI

- Quantum Encoding Techniques
- Quantum Feature Mapping for AI Models
- State Preparation for Machine Learning Tasks
- **Table:** Classical vs. Quantum Data Representation Methods

Chapter 6: Quantum Neural Networks (QNNs)

- Introduction to Quantum Perceptrons
- Variational Quantum Circuits in Deep Learning
- Training Quantum Neural Networks: Quantum Gradient Descent
- **Illustration:** Quantum Neural Network Architecture

PART III: BUILDING QUANTUM MACHINE LEARNING MODELS

Chapter 7: Quantum Supervised Learning Models

- Introduction to Supervised Learning in Quantum AI
- Quantum Support Vector Machines (QSVM)
- Quantum Decision Trees for Classification
- **Flowchart:** Workflow of Quantum Supervised Learning

Chapter 8: Quantum Unsupervised Learning Models

- Introduction to Unsupervised Learning in Quantum AI
- Quantum K-Means Clustering for Big Data
- Quantum Principal Component Analysis (QPCA)
- **Illustration:** Quantum Clustering vs. Classical Clustering

Chapter 9: Quantum Reinforcement Learning (QRL)

- The Basics of Reinforcement Learning
- How Quantum Agents Learn in QRL
- Quantum Markov Decision Processes
- **Case Study:** Quantum RL in Financial Optimization

PART IV: HANDS-ON QUANTUM MACHINE LEARNING WITH PYTHON

Chapter 10: Getting Started with Quantum Machine Learning

- Setting Up a QML Development Environment
- Installing and Configuring Qiskit, Cirq, and PennyLane
- Running Your First Quantum AI Model
- **Table:** Overview of QML Python Libraries

Chapter 11: Building a Quantum Classifier

- Step-by-Step Guide to Implementing a Quantum SVM
- Hybrid Quantum-Classical AI Models
- **Code Example:** Python Implementation of a Quantum Classifier

Chapter 12: Quantum Generative Adversarial Networks (Quantum GANs)

- Introduction to Generative Adversarial Networks
- How Quantum GANs Work
- Applications in Quantum Image Generation and Data Augmentation
- **Code Example:** Implementing a Quantum GAN using Qiskit

PART V: APPLICATIONS AND FUTURE OF QUANTUM MACHINE LEARNING

Chapter 13: Practical Applications of Quantum Machine Learning

- The Role of Quantum AI in Drug Discovery and Healthcare
- Financial Modeling and Quantum Risk Assessment
- The Impact of Quantum AI on Cybersecurity and Cryptography
- **Case Study:** Google's Quantum AI Research

Chapter 14: Challenges and Limitations of QML

- Hardware Limitations in Quantum AI Systems
- The Issue of Noisy Quantum Systems
- Quantum Error Correction Techniques
- **Table:** Comparison of Classical AI vs. Quantum AI - Limitations and Future Scope

Chapter 15: The Future of AI and Quantum Computing

- The Road to **Quantum Advantage** in AI
- Emerging Trends in Quantum AI Research
- Preparing for a Quantum AI Future
- Ethical Considerations and Security Risks in Quantum Machine Learning

Additional Resources

- **Appendix A:** Glossary of Quantum AI Terminology
- **Appendix B:** Quantum Computing and AI Research Papers
- **Appendix C:** Further Reading and Online Learning Resources

Chapter 1

Introduction to Artificial Intelligence and Machine Learning

The Evolution of Artificial Intelligence

Artificial Intelligence (AI) has come a long way since its early conceptualization. While today it powers some of the most complex technologies, AI's journey began with philosophical and mathematical inquiries centuries ago. The evolution of AI has been shaped by advances in computing power, data availability, and algorithmic innovations. To understand how AI has transformed into its current state, it is essential to explore its key milestones.

Early Foundations (Pre-20th Century)

Long before computers existed, philosophers and mathematicians speculated about the possibility of intelligent machines. Ancient Greek mythology included stories of automata—mechanical beings capable of performing tasks autonomously. The concept of machines that could mimic human intelligence was also explored in philosophical discussions.

One of the earliest formalizations of logical reasoning came from **Aristotle** in the 4th century BCE. His work laid the foundation for deductive reasoning, a critical component in AI. By the 17th and 18th centuries, mathematicians such as **René Descartes** and **Gottfried Wilhelm Leibniz** explored formal logic and mechanized reasoning.

Key Developments:

- **1642**: Blaise Pascal invented the Pascaline, an early mechanical calculator.
- **1673**: Leibniz developed a calculating machine that could perform basic arithmetic operations.
- **1854**: George Boole introduced Boolean algebra, a fundamental concept in AI and digital computing.

These developments showed that logical reasoning and computation could be represented mathematically, laying the groundwork for AI.

The Birth of Artificial Intelligence (1950s – 1970s)

The modern field of AI emerged in the 20th century with the advent of computers. Theoretical advancements and technological progress converged to create the first instances of artificial intelligence.

Key Milestones:

- **Alan Turing's Contributions (1950):** Turing proposed the **Turing Test**, a method to determine whether a machine can exhibit intelligent behavior indistinguishable from a human. His work on the **"Imitation Game"** set the stage for AI development.
- **1956 – The Dartmouth Conference:** The term **"Artificial Intelligence"** was formally coined by **John McCarthy** during the Dartmouth Conference. This event is widely regarded as the birth of AI as a distinct field of study.
- **Early AI Programs:**
    - **Logic Theorist (1956):** Created by Allen Newell and Herbert Simon, it could solve mathematical theorems.
    - **General Problem Solver (1957):** Designed to simulate human problem-solving processes.
- **1960s – Early AI Research:**
    - The first **chatbot**, ELIZA, was developed by Joseph Weizenbaum in 1966, demonstrating natural language processing (NLP).
    - The development of **expert systems**, which simulated decision-making, began to take shape.

Despite initial enthusiasm, AI faced significant challenges due to hardware limitations and inefficient algorithms, leading to the first **"AI Winter"** in the 1970s—a period of reduced funding and interest in AI research.

The Rise of Machine Learning (1980s – 1990s)

AI experienced a resurgence in the 1980s as researchers shifted focus from rule-based systems to machine learning approaches. The availability of more computing power and data allowed for statistical methods to gain traction.

Key Developments:

- **Expert Systems:** AI programs such as MYCIN and XCON helped in medical diagnostics and industrial applications.

- **Neural Networks Re-emergence:** The **backpropagation algorithm** allowed neural networks to be trained more efficiently, leading to renewed interest in AI.
- **The Shift to Data-Driven AI:** Researchers moved away from hand-coded rules and embraced **machine learning**, which focused on pattern recognition and learning from data.

By the 1990s, AI applications such as **speech recognition, computer vision, and recommendation systems** started to gain traction, although still in their infancy.

The AI Revolution (2000s – Present)

With the explosion of big data, advanced algorithms, and powerful computing resources, AI entered an era of rapid expansion.

Key Events:

- **2006 – Deep Learning Renaissance:** Geoffrey Hinton and his team reintroduced deep learning, leading to breakthroughs in AI capabilities.
- **2011 – IBM Watson Defeats Humans on Jeopardy!:** Watson's ability to process natural language and answer complex questions showcased AI's growing capabilities.
- **2012 – ImageNet Challenge:** Deep learning models outperformed traditional computer vision techniques, marking a turning point in AI research.
- **2016 – AlphaGo Defeats a Human Champion:** Google DeepMind's AlphaGo defeated the world champion Go player, demonstrating the power of AI in strategic decision-making.
- **Recent Advances:** AI now powers **autonomous vehicles, medical diagnostics, voice assistants (Alexa, Siri), and generative AI models (GPT, DALL-E, MidJourney).**

Today, AI is at the forefront of scientific, industrial, and commercial innovation, with new applications emerging at an unprecedented pace.

Machine Learning vs. Deep Learning: Key Differences

Machine learning and deep learning are two fundamental branches of AI. While they share similarities, they differ in **complexity, approach, and capabilities**.

1. Definition and Core Concept

- **Machine Learning (ML):** A subset of AI that enables computers to learn from data without being explicitly programmed. It relies on statistical models and algorithms.
- **Deep Learning (DL):** A subset of ML that uses neural networks with multiple layers (**deep neural networks**) to learn complex patterns from large datasets.

2. Learning Process

Feature	Machine Learning	Deep Learning
Feature Engineering	Requires manual feature selection	Automatically learns features
Data Dependency	Works well with small to medium-sized datasets	Requires massive datasets
Model Complexity	Uses decision trees, SVMs, and linear regression	Uses deep neural networks (CNNs, RNNs)
Processing Power	Less computationally expensive	Requires high-performance GPUs and TPUs
Interpretability	More interpretable	Often considered a "black box"

3. Applications

- **Machine Learning:**
  - Fraud Detection
  - Spam Filtering
  - Recommendation Systems
- **Deep Learning:**
  - Image and Speech Recognition
  - Natural Language Processing
  - Autonomous Vehicles

4

Deep learning surpasses traditional ML in performance for tasks like **computer vision and NLP**, but it requires vast computing resources.

The Role of AI in Modern Technology

AI is transforming nearly every industry, enhancing efficiency and enabling **new capabilities** that were previously impossible.

1. Healthcare and Medicine

- AI-driven diagnostics detect diseases like **cancer** with high accuracy.
- Personalized medicine tailors treatments based on **genetic data**.
- **AI-powered drug discovery** accelerates vaccine and pharmaceutical development.

2. Finance and Banking

- Fraud detection algorithms identify suspicious transactions.
- AI-powered trading bots optimize stock market strategies.
- **Chatbots and virtual assistants** enhance customer service.

3. Autonomous Systems and Robotics

- Self-driving cars utilize AI for navigation and decision-making.
- AI-powered robots assist in manufacturing and logistics.
- **Drones and robotics** are used in military and emergency response.

4. Natural Language Processing (NLP)

- AI chatbots and virtual assistants like **Siri, Alexa, and ChatGPT** improve human-computer interaction.
- Sentiment analysis and **automated translations** break language barriers.

5. Cybersecurity

- AI detects **cyber threats and vulnerabilities** in real-time.
- Machine learning models predict and prevent attacks before they occur.

6. Entertainment and Media

- AI-powered recommendation systems (Netflix, Spotify) personalize user experiences.
- Generative AI creates **realistic deepfake videos, artwork, and music.**

7. Scientific Research and Space Exploration

- AI assists in **protein folding simulations**, helping understand diseases.
- NASA uses AI for **Mars rover navigation and space mission planning.**

AI is reshaping modern technology, and as **quantum computing** advances, AI's potential will expand even further.

This **comprehensive section** ensures a strong foundation in **AI's evolution, ML vs. DL, and its role in modern technology**, preparing readers for the intersection of **Quantum Machine Learning** in later chapters

Why Traditional AI Faces Limitations

Artificial Intelligence has advanced significantly over the decades, powering everything from **autonomous systems** to **personalized recommendations**. However, despite these remarkable achievements, **traditional AI—built on classical computing principles—faces inherent limitations** that hinder its ability to tackle more complex problems efficiently. These limitations primarily arise from constraints in **computational power, scalability, data efficiency, interpretability, and energy consumption.**

Quantum computing is emerging as a potential game-changer, offering new computational paradigms that could **overcome many of AI's current limitations**. To understand why traditional AI struggles with certain challenges, we need to explore its key limitations in depth.

1. The Computational Bottleneck

Traditional AI models rely on **classical computers**, which process information using **binary logic (bits: 0s and 1s)**. While modern processors are **incredibly powerful**, they still struggle with certain tasks that require **exponential computing power**.

Challenges in High-Dimensional Data Processing

- **Deep learning models require immense computational resources.** Training a large neural network like GPT-4 can take **weeks** on high-end **GPU clusters**.
- **Simulating complex systems**, such as **molecular interactions, climate models, and cryptographic algorithms**, requires enormous computational effort that even supercomputers struggle with.
- **Hyperparameter optimization**—a key component in deep learning—requires numerous trial-and-error cycles, making model training inefficient.

These computational constraints limit AI's ability to **scale efficiently** and force researchers to **trade off between model accuracy and performance**.

Why Quantum Computing Helps

Quantum computing operates on **quantum bits (qubits)**, which **leverage superposition and entanglement** to process multiple computations **simultaneously**. This parallelism enables quantum computers to **analyze complex patterns exponentially faster**, making them **ideal for large-scale AI applications**.

---

2. Data Dependency and Generalization Issues

Traditional AI's Need for Big Data

Machine learning models—particularly deep learning—require **massive datasets** to perform well. The effectiveness of AI often depends on:

- The **quantity and quality** of training data.
- **Well-labeled datasets** for supervised learning.
- **Data augmentation techniques** to improve performance in low-data scenarios.

However, real-world applications often suffer from **data scarcity**, which reduces model reliability. Many industries—such as **healthcare, security, and quantum physics**—lack sufficient labeled datasets, making AI model training **challenging and expensive**.

Why Quantum AI Helps

Quantum computing introduces new methods of **data representation and feature encoding**, making it possible to learn from fewer data points. Quantum-enhanced machine learning models can:

- **Extract hidden correlations** in smaller datasets.
- **Leverage quantum probability distributions** for improved generalization.
- **Reduce the dependency on large-scale labeled datasets** by encoding more information per qubit.

These advantages make **Quantum AI** more suitable for fields where **data collection is difficult or expensive**, such as **drug discovery, material science, and cryptography**.

---

3. Model Interpretability and Explainability Challenges

Traditional AI as a "Black Box"

- Deep learning models—especially deep neural networks (DNNs)—are **highly complex** and lack interpretability.
- AI-powered **medical diagnostics, finance, and legal decision-making** require explainable models, yet most traditional AI methods fail to provide transparent decision-making.
- Regulatory frameworks (such as **GDPR**) demand AI models to justify decisions, posing challenges for deep learning adoption in **high-risk industries**.

Why Quantum AI Helps

Quantum computing enables **alternative AI architectures** that **reduce model complexity** while preserving high accuracy. **Quantum-inspired decision trees and explainable quantum kernels** provide:

- **Better interpretability of AI models.**
- **More transparent decision-making frameworks.**
- **Lower risk in critical applications like AI-driven healthcare.**

This **enhanced explainability** makes Quantum AI more practical for industries where **transparency is mandatory**.

4. Energy Consumption and Efficiency

The Energy Problem in AI Training

Training deep learning models consumes enormous amounts of energy.

- **GPT-4 requires thousands of GPUs running continuously for weeks.**
- AI training **carbon emissions** are equivalent to those produced by multiple cars in their lifetime.
- **Supercomputers** are essential for AI research, but they **consume megawatts of power**, making AI **unsustainable at scale**.

Why Quantum AI Helps

Quantum computers **process information differently**, reducing computational complexity and energy requirements.

- **Quantum parallelism reduces training time significantly.**
- **Lower energy consumption for large-scale AI tasks.**
- **Quantum algorithms require fewer operations compared to classical approaches.**

By reducing energy costs, **Quantum AI makes AI research more sustainable**, leading to **faster and more eco-friendly innovations**.

5. Limitations in Solving Certain AI Problems

Traditional AI struggles with:

- **Combinatorial Optimization Problems:** Finding the best solution among exponentially growing possibilities (e.g., logistics, cryptography, drug design).
- **Quantum Simulation Tasks:** AI cannot efficiently simulate quantum states using classical hardware.
- **High-Dimensional Probability Distributions:** AI models struggle with probabilistic modeling when complexity increases.

Quantum AI overcomes these challenges by leveraging **quantum parallelism**, enabling:

9

- **More efficient combinatorial optimization (e.g., traffic routing, logistics).**
- **Better probability estimation using quantum probability models.**
- **Faster simulation of quantum systems (e.g., material discovery, cryptographic security).**

These advantages position Quantum AI as a **revolutionary leap** beyond traditional AI.

Table: Classical vs. Quantum AI Approaches

Feature	Classical AI	Quantum AI
Computation Type	Binary (0s and 1s)	Quantum bits (qubits) leveraging superposition and entanglement
Processing Power	Limited by Moore's Law and hardware constraints	Quantum parallelism enables massive speed-up
Data Requirements	Requires large datasets for accuracy	Can learn from fewer data points using quantum feature encoding
Energy Consumption	High, requires large computing clusters	Lower, more efficient for large-scale computations
Algorithm Performance	Slower for high-dimensional optimization tasks	Faster at solving complex problems (e.g., combinatorial optimization)
Interpretability	Many deep learning models are black-box	Quantum-inspired AI models allow better interpretability

Simulation Capabilities	Cannot efficiently simulate quantum systems	Naturally suited for quantum simulations and material science
Cybersecurit y Impact	Vulnerable to advanced cryptographic attacks	Quantum AI can break classical cryptography but also enable quantum-secure encryption
Real-World Applications	Used in NLP, computer vision, fraud detection, etc.	Ideal for optimization problems, scientific computing, and cryptography
Scalability	Limited by classical computing power	Scales better for complex AI tasks using quantum resources

Quantum computing offers a paradigm shift in how AI models operate. By addressing the **fundamental limitations** of traditional AI, **Quantum AI can unlock new capabilities** in machine learning, optimization, and data processing.

As we move toward the era of **Quantum Machine Learning**, it is crucial to **understand how quantum mechanics and AI can be combined** to push the boundaries of computation. The next chapters will explore **Quantum Data Representation, Quantum Neural Networks, and Practical Applications of Quantum AI**.

Chapter 2

Introduction to Quantum Computing

Quantum computing represents a **paradigm shift** in the way we process and manipulate information. Unlike classical computing, which relies on binary states (0s and 1s), quantum computing leverages the unique properties of **quantum mechanics** to perform computations in ways that were once thought impossible. These principles—**superposition, entanglement, and interference**—allow quantum computers to **process massive amounts of information exponentially faster** than classical systems.

As we delve into the world of **Quantum Computing**, we will first define what it is, compare it with classical computing, and explore its fundamental principles.

What is Quantum Computing?

Quantum computing is an advanced computing paradigm that utilizes the principles of **quantum mechanics** to solve complex problems significantly faster than classical computers. While classical computers operate using **bits** (0s and 1s), quantum computers use **qubits (quantum bits)**, which can exist in **multiple states simultaneously** due to a phenomenon called **superposition**. Additionally, qubits can become **entangled**, allowing them to share information instantaneously regardless of distance.

Quantum computing is not just an incremental improvement over classical computing—it represents an entirely **new way of processing information**, with the potential to revolutionize fields such as **artificial intelligence, cryptography, materials science, and financial modeling**.

How Quantum Computing Works

At the core of quantum computing are **qubits**, which function very differently from classical bits. Quantum computers use **quantum gates** to manipulate qubits, similar to how classical computers use logic gates. However, these quantum gates take advantage of **superposition, entanglement, and quantum interference** to perform complex calculations more efficiently.

Key Components of a Quantum Computer

1. **Qubits** – The fundamental unit of quantum information, analogous to bits in classical computing.
2. **Quantum Gates** – Operations that change the state of qubits, enabling computation.
3. **Quantum Circuits** – A series of quantum gates applied to qubits to perform calculations.
4. **Quantum Decoherence Management** – Mechanisms to maintain quantum states against noise and instability.
5. **Cryogenic Cooling Systems** – Most quantum computers operate at **near absolute zero** to maintain quantum coherence.

Quantum computers use **quantum parallelism** to evaluate multiple possibilities at once, making them particularly powerful for **optimization, cryptography, and artificial intelligence**.

Classical vs. Quantum Computing: A Comparative Analysis

Quantum computing and classical computing are fundamentally different in their approach to processing information. While classical computers have been the backbone of technological advancements for decades, quantum computers introduce a **new dimension of computation** that goes beyond traditional binary logic.

Key Differences Between Classical and Quantum Computing

Feature	Classical Computing	Quantum Computing
Data Representation	Uses **bits** (0s and 1s)	Uses **qubits**, which can exist in superposition (0 and 1 simultaneously)
Processing Speed	Executes computations **sequentially** or in parallel using multi-threading	Uses **quantum parallelism**, processing multiple computations at once

Computational Power	Scales linearly with hardware improvements (follows **Moore's Law**)	Can achieve **exponential speed-up** for certain problems
Logic Operations	Uses **Boolean logic gates** (AND, OR, NOT)	Uses **quantum gates** (Hadamard, Pauli-X, CNOT, etc.)
Memory	Stores information explicitly (one state per bit)	Stores multiple states at once using superposition
Communication	Follows classical data transfer methods	Uses **quantum teleportation and entanglement** for instantaneous information sharing
Error Sensitivity	Errors can be corrected with redundancy and checksum methods	Requires **quantum error correction** due to decoherence
Cryptography	Uses RSA encryption (relies on factorization difficulty)	Can break RSA encryption using **Shor's Algorithm**
Applications	Used for general-purpose computing, AI, gaming, business applications, etc.	Best suited for **optimization, cryptography, material simulation, AI, and quantum chemistry**

While classical computers remain **indispensable** for everyday computing tasks, **quantum computing is poised to revolutionize problem-solving in areas where classical methods struggle**.

Fundamental Principles of Quantum Computing

14

Quantum computing relies on several fundamental principles that differentiate it from classical computing. These principles—**superposition, entanglement, and interference**—are what enable quantum computers to achieve their extraordinary computational power.

---

1. Superposition: The Power of Multiple States

Superposition is one of the most defining principles of quantum mechanics. In classical computing, a **bit** can exist in **only one state at a time**—either 0 or 1. However, a **qubit can exist in both states simultaneously** due to superposition.

How Superposition Works

- If a **classical bit** represents **0 or 1**, a **qubit** can represent **0, 1, or any quantum combination of both simultaneously**.
- When a quantum algorithm runs, it **processes all possible states at once**, leading to an **exponential increase in computing power**.

Example of Superposition in Computing

Imagine a classical computer trying to solve a maze. It must check each possible path **one by one** until it finds the correct route. In contrast, a quantum computer—leveraging superposition—**evaluates all paths simultaneously**, drastically speeding up problem-solving.

Mathematical Representation

A qubit's state is described as a **linear combination (superposition) of basis states**:

$$|\psi\rangle = \alpha|0\rangle + \beta|1\rangle$$

where α and β are probability amplitudes that determine the likelihood of measuring 0 or 1 when observed.

Superposition is what allows **quantum parallelism**, enabling quantum computers to **outperform classical computers in specific tasks**.

---

2. Entanglement: Instantaneous Correlation Across Space

Entanglement is another revolutionary concept in quantum mechanics. When two qubits become **entangled**, their states become **interdependent**, meaning that measuring one qubit **instantly determines the state of the other—regardless of distance**.

How Entanglement Works

- If two qubits are entangled, they form a **single quantum system**.
- Changing one qubit **immediately affects the other**, even if they are light-years apart.
- Einstein famously called this phenomenon **"spooky action at a distance"** because it defied classical intuitions about locality.

Example of Quantum Entanglement

If a pair of entangled qubits is created, one may be in state $|0\rangle$ and the other in $|1\rangle$. However, their individual states remain **undefined until measured**. If one qubit collapses to $|0\rangle$, the other **instantaneously collapses to $|1\rangle$**, no matter how far apart they are.

Mathematical Representation of an Entangled State

$$|\Phi^+\rangle = \frac{1}{\sqrt{2}} (|00\rangle + |11\rangle)$$

This means that if one qubit is measured as **0**, the other **must** be 0 as well. If one is measured as **1**, the other must be 1.

Applications of Entanglement

- **Quantum Cryptography:** Entanglement ensures secure communication through **Quantum Key Distribution (QKD)**.
- **Quantum Networking:** Enables quantum computers to share information instantaneously.
- **Teleportation of Information:** Quantum teleportation allows information transfer without direct transmission.

Entanglement is **one of the most powerful features** of quantum computing, enabling communication and computing capabilities that classical systems cannot replicate.

Quantum computing introduces **a new way of thinking about computation** by harnessing the principles of **superposition and entanglement**. Unlike classical computing, which processes information sequentially, quantum computing operates on **multiple possibilities simultaneously**, unlocking **unprecedented computing power**.

As we progress, we will explore **Quantum Gates, Quantum Circuits, and the impact of Quantum Computing on Artificial Intelligence**, further revealing how **Quantum Machine Learning** is set to transform the future of AI.

Overview of Quantum Gates and Circuits

Quantum gates and circuits are fundamental building blocks of **quantum computing**, analogous to logic gates in classical computing. However, unlike classical gates that process **binary bits (0 and 1) using Boolean logic**, quantum gates manipulate **qubits** by leveraging **quantum superposition, entanglement, and interference**.

Understanding **quantum gates and circuits** is essential to grasp **how quantum computers execute algorithms, process information, and enable advanced applications in AI and machine learning**.

---

1. Understanding Quantum Gates

What Are Quantum Gates?

A **quantum gate** is a mathematical operation applied to one or more **qubits**, transforming their quantum state. These gates perform **reversible transformations** (unlike classical logic gates, which can be irreversible).

In classical computing, basic logic gates include **AND, OR, NOT, XOR**, and others. In quantum computing, **quantum gates perform more complex transformations**, allowing computations that classical computers cannot efficiently perform.

Characteristics of Quantum Gates

- **Reversible Operations** – Unlike classical gates (such as NAND), all quantum gates are unitary operations, meaning they can be undone by applying their inverse.

- **Probabilistic Nature** – Quantum gates manipulate probability amplitudes, meaning measurement collapses the qubit to a specific state probabilistically.
- **Multi-Qubit Interactions** – Some quantum gates operate on multiple qubits, enabling entanglement and advanced quantum operations.

---

2. Common Types of Quantum Gates

Quantum Gate	Symbol	Description	Mathematical Representation
Pauli-X (X Gate)	XXX	Equivalent to classical NOT gate, flips	0⟩ to
Pauli-Y (Y Gate)	YYY	Rotates the qubit around the Y-axis	Y=[0−ii0]Y = \begin{bmatrix} 0 & -i \\ i & 0 \end{bmatrix}Y=[0i−i0]
Pauli-Z (Z Gate)	ZZZ	Flips the phase of	1⟩ while leaving
Hadamard (H Gate)	HHH	Creates superposition (0⟩ +	1⟩ states)
CNOT (Controlled-NOT)	CNOT CNOT CNOT	Flips target qubit if control qubit is	1⟩
SWAP Gate	SWAP SWAP SWAP	Swaps the states of two qubits	SWAP=[100000100100 0001]SWAP = \begin{bmatrix} 1 & 0 & 0 & 0 \\ 0 & 0 & 1 & 0 \\ 0 & 1 & 0 & 0 \\ 0 & 0 & 0 & 1 \end{bmatrix}SWAP=10 00001001000001

Toffoli Gate	CCNO TCCN OTCC NOT	Classical AND gate equivalent, reversible	Three-qubit operation

Quantum gates **enable powerful quantum algorithms** by manipulating qubit states. These gates are **combined in sequences** to form **quantum circuits**.

Illustration: Quantum Circuit Representation

A **quantum circuit** is a sequence of quantum gates applied to a set of qubits to perform computations. It is similar to **electronic circuits in classical computing**, but instead of processing bits, it manipulates **qubits using quantum gates**.

Basic Structure of a Quantum Circuit

A **quantum circuit** consists of:

1. **Quantum Registers** – A collection of qubits used in computation.
2. **Quantum Gates** – Operations applied to qubits to perform calculations.
3. **Measurement Operations** – Converts quantum states into classical bits after computation.

Below is a **simple quantum circuit diagram** illustrating an **entanglement operation** using Hadamard and CNOT gates:

yaml
CopyEdit

```
Qubit 0: |0⟩ ———H———o———
                      |
Qubit 1: |0⟩ ————————X———
```

How This Circuit Works:

1. **Hadamard (H) Gate** – Places **Qubit 0** in **superposition** (equal probability of |0⟩ and |1⟩).
2. **CNOT Gate** – Entangles **Qubit 1** with Qubit 0, creating an **entangled Bell state**.

After execution, measuring these qubits will always result in **correlated outcomes**, demonstrating quantum entanglement.

The Power of Quantum Parallelism in AI

One of the **greatest strengths** of quantum computing is **quantum parallelism**, which enables **exponential computational speed-up**. Unlike classical computers that process **one computation at a time**, quantum computers can **explore multiple solutions simultaneously**.

How Quantum Parallelism Works

- **Superposition enables qubits to exist in multiple states at once**.
- A quantum computer can evaluate **all possible solutions simultaneously**, rather than checking them **one by one**.
- Quantum gates **interfere** with different computational paths, allowing the algorithm to emphasize the **correct solutions** while canceling incorrect ones.

Impact of Quantum Parallelism on AI

AI Task	Classical Computing	Quantum Computing
Training Deep Learning Models	Requires **massive labeled datasets** and long computation times	Can accelerate **training using quantum feature mapping**

Optimization Problems	Exponential time complexity for large datasets	Quantum algorithms explore **all solutions simultaneously**
Big Data Processing	Slower with increasing dataset size	**Processes vast datasets efficiently** using quantum-enhanced search
Natural Language Processing (NLP)	Requires **large-scale recurrent networks**	Quantum NLP uses **quantum word embeddings** for efficient learning
AI-powered Drug Discovery	Requires **supercomputing resources**	Quantum AI can **simulate molecular interactions exponentially faster**

Example: Quantum Speed-up in AI

1. **Quantum Search Algorithms (Grover's Algorithm)**

   - Classical search requires **O(N) time complexity** for an unsorted dataset.
   - **Quantum search reduces complexity to O($\sqrt{N}$),** providing quadratic speed-up.
2. **Quantum Machine Learning (QML)**

   - Quantum computers can **learn from fewer data points** using quantum feature space.
   - QML improves **clustering, classification, and generative modeling** beyond classical capabilities.

Case Study: Quantum AI in Finance

- **Quantum-enhanced AI** is being tested in **financial portfolio optimization**, where **Monte Carlo simulations** take days on classical supercomputers.
- **Quantum computing reduces computation time from days to seconds**, enabling **real-time risk analysis**.

Quantum computing introduces **quantum gates and circuits** that **process information fundamentally differently** from classical systems. By leveraging **superposition and entanglement**, quantum circuits enable **quantum parallelism**, making AI models **faster, more efficient, and capable of handling previously intractable problems**.

The next sections will explore **Quantum Data Representation, Quantum Neural Networks, and real-world applications of Quantum Machine Learning**, further bridging the connection between **Quantum Computing and Artificial Intelligence**.

Chapter 3

Mathematical Foundations of Quantum Machine Learning

Quantum Machine Learning (QML) combines quantum computing principles with artificial intelligence, leveraging quantum mechanics to create **faster, more efficient AI models**. However, to understand how QML operates, it is essential to grasp its **mathematical foundations**, which rely heavily on **linear algebra, quantum states, wave functions, and quantum probability theory**.

This chapter provides a **comprehensive mathematical framework** to understand **Quantum Machine Learning**, covering key topics such as **linear algebra in quantum computing, quantum states and wave functions, and quantum probability and measurement**.

Essential Linear Algebra for Quantum Computing

1. The Role of Linear Algebra in Quantum Computing

Linear algebra plays a **crucial role** in quantum computing because **quantum states, quantum gates, and measurements** are represented using matrices and vectors. **Operations on qubits** are performed through matrix multiplications, making linear algebra the **foundation of quantum algorithms**.

2. Key Linear Algebra Concepts for Quantum Computing

Vectors and Vector Spaces

- A **vector** is an ordered set of numbers representing a quantum state.

- Quantum states are described as **vectors in a Hilbert space** (complex vector space).

- **Example:** A single qubit can be represented as:
  $|\psi\rangle=\begin{bmatrix} a \\ b \end{bmatrix}, where a, b \in C$ | \psi \rangle = \begin{bmatrix} a \\ b \end{bmatrix},

$\quad \text{where} \quad a, b \in \mathbb{C} \, |\psi\rangle=[ab]$, where $a,b \in C$

The coefficients aaa and bbb are **complex numbers** and determine the probability of measuring the qubit in a particular state.

Matrix Representation of Quantum Operators

- Quantum gates are **unitary matrices** that operate on quantum states.

- A matrix **UUU** is unitary if:
  $U\dagger U = I U^\dagger U = I U\dagger U = I$
  where $U\dagger U^\dagger U\dagger$ is the conjugate transpose of UUU, and III is the identity matrix.

- Example: The Hadamard Gate, which creates **superposition**, is represented as:
  $H=\frac{1}{2}[11 1 {-}1] H = \frac{1}{\sqrt{2}} \begin{bmatrix} 1 & 1 \\ 1 & -1 \end{bmatrix} H = \frac{1}{2}[11 1 {-}1]$

Inner Product and Outer Product

- The **inner product** between two vectors $|\psi\rangle$ | \psi \rangle $|\psi\rangle$ and $|\phi\rangle$ | \phi \rangle $|\phi\rangle$ is given by:
  $\langle\psi|\phi\rangle=\sum_i a_i{*}b_i \langle \psi | \phi \rangle = \sum_{i} a_i^* b_i \langle\psi|\phi\rangle=\sum a_i{*}b_i$
  where $a_i{*}a_i^{**}a_i{*}$ is the **complex conjugate** of $a_i a\_iai$.

- The **outer product** is used in quantum measurement operations:
  $|\psi\rangle\langle\phi| | \psi \rangle \langle \phi | |\psi\rangle\langle\phi|$
  This forms a **projection matrix**, which is essential in quantum measurements.

Tensor Products and Multi-Qubit Systems

- The **tensor product** allows multiple qubits to be represented as a single quantum system.

- If two qubits have states:
  $|\psi 1\rangle=[ab], |\psi 2\rangle=[cd] | \psi_1 \rangle = \begin{bmatrix} a \\ b \end{bmatrix}, \quad | \psi_2 \rangle = \begin{bmatrix} c \\ d \end{bmatrix} |\psi 1\rangle=[ab], |\psi 2\rangle=[cd]$
  Their combined state is:
  $|\psi 1\rangle\otimes|\psi 2\rangle=[ab]\otimes[cd]=[acadbcbd] | \psi_1 \rangle \otimes | \psi_2 \rangle =$

\begin{bmatrix} a \\ b \end{bmatrix} \otimes \begin{bmatrix} c \\ d
\end{bmatrix} = \begin{bmatrix} ac \\ ad \\ bc \\ bd
\end{bmatrix}|ψ1⟩⊗|ψ2⟩=[ab]⊗[cd]=acadbcbd

This property enables **entanglement** and complex quantum algorithms.

Quantum States and Wave Functions

1. What is a Quantum State?

A **quantum state** describes the properties of a **quantum system** and provides all possible information about a quantum particle. Quantum states are represented using **wave functions** or **state vectors**.

In the **Dirac notation**, a quantum state is written as:

$|ψ⟩|$ \psi \rangle $|ψ⟩$

which represents a **vector in a complex vector space**.

2. Representation of a Qubit

A single qubit has two possible basis states, labeled as:

$|0⟩=[10],|1⟩=[01]|$ 0 \rangle = \begin{bmatrix} 1 \\ 0 \end{bmatrix}, \quad | 1 \rangle = \begin{bmatrix} 0 \\ 1 \end{bmatrix}$|0⟩=[10],|1⟩=[01]$

A **general qubit state** is a **linear combination (superposition)** of these basis states:

$|ψ⟩=α|0⟩+β|1⟩|$ \psi \rangle = \alpha | 0 \rangle + \beta | 1 \rangle $|ψ⟩=α|0⟩+β|1⟩$

where **α\alphaα** and **β\betaβ** are complex numbers satisfying the normalization condition:

$|α|2+|β|2=1|$\alpha|^2 + |\beta|^2 = 1 $|α|2+|β|2=1$

This ensures that the total probability of measuring the qubit in **either state** is **1**.

3. Quantum Wave Function

In quantum mechanics, a **wave function $\Psi(x,t)$\Psi(x,t)$\Psi(x,t)$** describes the quantum state of a system. The probability of finding a particle at position xxx is given by:

$P(x)=|\Psi(x,t)|2P(x) = |\Psi(x,t)|^2P(x)=|\Psi(x,t)|2$

which follows the **Born Rule**. The wave function is a **complex-valued function**, allowing it to describe **probabilistic quantum behavior**.

Quantum Probability and Measurement

1. The Concept of Quantum Measurement

In classical probability theory, measuring a system reveals an exact value. However, **quantum measurement is probabilistic**, meaning it **collapses** a superposition state into one of the possible classical states.

When a quantum state is **measured**, it collapses into **either** $|0\rangle|0\rangle|0\rangle$ or $|1\rangle|1\rangle|1\rangle$, with probabilities determined by $|\alpha|2|\alpha|^2|\alpha|2$ and $|\beta|2|\beta|^2|\beta|2$.

2. Probability Amplitudes and the Born Rule

The **Born Rule** states that the probability of measuring a quantum state in a particular basis state is given by:

$P(|0\rangle)=|\alpha|2,P(|1\rangle)=|\beta|2P(|0\rangle) = |\alpha|^2, \quad P(|1\rangle) = |\beta|^2P(|0\rangle)=|\alpha|2,P(|1\rangle)=|\beta|2$

where $\alpha\alpha\alpha$ and $\beta\beta\beta$ are **complex probability amplitudes**.

3. Example: Measuring a Superposition State

Consider a qubit in the state:

$|\psi\rangle=13|0\rangle+23|1\rangle|\psi \rangle = \frac{1}{\sqrt{3}} |0\rangle + \frac{2}{\sqrt{3}} |1\rangle|\psi\rangle=31|0\rangle+32|1\rangle$

The probability of measuring $|0\rangle|0\rangle|0\rangle$ is:

$P(0)=|13|2=13P(0) = \left| \frac{1}{\sqrt{3}} \right|^2 = \frac{1}{3}P(0)=312=31$

26

The probability of measuring $|1\rangle$ is:

$$P(1) = \left| \frac{2}{\sqrt{3}} \right|^2 = \frac{4}{3}$$

Thus, if measured, the qubit **collapses** to $|0\rangle$ with **probability 1/3** or $|1\rangle$ with **probability 2/3**.

4. Quantum Measurement Operators

Quantum measurement is described by **projection operators**. Given a quantum state:

$$|\psi\rangle = \alpha |0\rangle + \beta |1\rangle$$

The measurement operator for $|0\rangle$ is:

$$M_0 = |0\rangle \langle 0|$$

The probability of measuring **0** is:

$$P(0) = \langle \psi | M_0 | \psi \rangle$$

Similarly, for $|1\rangle$:

$$P(1) = \langle \psi | M_1 | \psi \rangle$$

where $M_1 = |1\rangle \langle 1|$.

This section establishes the **mathematical foundation** for quantum machine learning, providing a deep understanding of **linear algebra, quantum states, wave functions, and quantum probability**. These concepts are essential for **building and understanding quantum AI models**.

The next sections will explore **Quantum Fourier Transform, Quantum Neural Networks, and how these mathematical principles apply to real-world Quantum Machine Learning tasks**.

Tensor Notation in Quantum Computation

1. Understanding Tensor Notation in Quantum Computing

Tensor notation is a **powerful mathematical framework** used to describe **multi-qubit quantum systems**. Since quantum computing operates in **high-dimensional vector spaces**, tensor notation provides a structured way to **represent, manipulate, and compute quantum states efficiently**.

In classical computing, a system of multiple bits is simply represented by their individual binary values. However, in quantum computing, multiple qubits exist in **superposition and entanglement**, requiring **tensor products** to represent their combined state.

---

2. Single Qubit States and Tensor Notation

A single qubit state is typically written as:

$|\psi\rangle = \alpha|0\rangle + \beta|1\rangle$

where **α\alphaα** and **β\betaβ** are complex probability amplitudes.

For a **multi-qubit system**, we use the **tensor product (⊗)** to describe the full quantum state.

---

3. Multi-Qubit Systems Using Tensor Products

When dealing with multiple qubits, we must compute their **combined quantum state** using the **tensor product (⊗)** of individual qubit states.

For a **two-qubit system**, where **Qubit 1** is in state:

$|\psi_1\rangle = a|0\rangle + b|1\rangle$

and **Qubit 2** is in state:

$|\psi_2\rangle = c|0\rangle + d|1\rangle$

Their **combined state** is given by the tensor product:
28

$|\psi\rangle=|\psi1\rangle\otimes|\psi2\rangle| \psi \rangle = | \psi_1 \rangle \otimes | \psi_2 \rangle|\psi\rangle=|\psi1\rangle\otimes|\psi2\rangle$ $=(a|0\rangle+b|1\rangle)\otimes(c|0\rangle+d|1\rangle)= (a |0\rangle + b |1\rangle) \otimes (c |0\rangle + d |1\rangle)=(a|0\rangle+b|1\rangle)\otimes(c|0\rangle+d|1\rangle) =ac|00\rangle+ad|01\rangle+bc|10\rangle+bd|11\rangle= ac |00\rangle + ad |01\rangle + bc |10\rangle + bd |11\rangle=ac|00\rangle+ad|01\rangle+bc|10\rangle+bd|11\rangle$

This equation shows that a **two-qubit system exists in four possible states simultaneously**, enabling quantum parallelism.

For a **three-qubit system**, the tensor product expands further:

$|\psi\rangle=|\psi1\rangle\otimes|\psi2\rangle\otimes|\psi3\rangle| \psi \rangle = | \psi_1 \rangle \otimes | \psi_2 \rangle \otimes | \psi_3 \rangle|\psi\rangle=|\psi1\rangle\otimes|\psi2\rangle\otimes|\psi3\rangle =(a1|0\rangle+b1|1\rangle)\otimes(a2|0\rangle+b2|1\rangle)\otimes(a3|0\rangle+b3|1\rangle)= (a_1 |0\rangle + b_1 |1\rangle) \otimes (a_2 |0\rangle + b_2 |1\rangle) \otimes (a_3 |0\rangle + b_3 |1\rangle)=(a1|0\rangle+b1|1\rangle)\otimes(a2|0\rangle+b2|1\rangle)\otimes(a3|0\rangle+b3|1\rangle)$ $=a1a2a3|000\rangle+a1a2b3|001\rangle+a1b2a3|010\rangle+...+b1b2b3|111\rangle= a_1 a_2 a_3 |000\rangle + a_1 a_2 b_3 |001\rangle + a_1 b_2 a_3 |010\rangle + ... + b_1 b_2 b_3 |111\rangle=a1a2a3|000\rangle+a1a2b3|001\rangle+a1b2a3|010\rangle+...+b1b2b3|111\rangle$

This **exponential state expansion** enables quantum computing to process a vast number of possible states simultaneously, making it ideal for AI and machine learning applications.

---

4. Tensor Notation for Quantum Gates

Quantum gates also follow **tensor notation** when applied to multi-qubit systems.

For example, the **Hadamard gate (H)** applied to a single qubit:

$H=12[111-1]H = \frac{1}{\sqrt{2}} \begin{bmatrix} 1 & 1 \\ 1 & -1 \end{bmatrix}H=21[111-1]$

For a **two-qubit system**, applying Hadamard to both qubits requires the **tensor product**:

$H\otimes H=12[11111-11-111-1-11-1-11]H \otimes H = \frac{1}{2} \begin{bmatrix} 1 & 1 & 1 & 1 \\ 1 & -1 & 1 & -1 \\ 1 & 1 & -1 & -1 \\ 1 & -1 & -1 & 1 \end{bmatrix}H\otimes H=2111111-11-111-1-11-1-11$

This expanded matrix describes how the Hadamard transformation applies to **both qubits simultaneously**, enabling **superposition and parallel computation**.

Introduction to the Quantum Fourier Transform (QFT)

1. What is the Quantum Fourier Transform?

The **Quantum Fourier Transform (QFT)** is the quantum equivalent of the **Discrete Fourier Transform (DFT)**, widely used in **signal processing, cryptography, and AI**. It is a key mathematical tool in **quantum algorithms**, enabling efficient solutions to **factoring, period finding, and quantum AI applications**.

Mathematically, the QFT transforms a quantum state **from one basis to another** using **complex phase factors**.

2. Mathematical Definition of the QFT

For an **N-dimensional quantum state**, the **QFT transforms** a quantum state $|x\rangle$ into another quantum state $|y\rangle$ as follows:

$$QFT(|x\rangle) = \frac{1}{\sqrt{N}} \sum_{y=0}^{N-1} e^{2\pi i xy / N} |y\rangle$$

where:

- N is the total number of quantum states.
- $e^{2\pi i xy / N}$ represents a **complex phase factor**.

The QFT is **reversible**, meaning that applying the inverse QFT **retrieves the original quantum state**.

3. QFT on a Two-Qubit System

For a **two-qubit quantum state**:

$|\psi\rangle = a_0 |00\rangle + a_1 |01\rangle + a_2 |10\rangle + a_3 |11\rangle$

Applying the **QFT** transforms this into:

$|\psi'\rangle = \frac{1}{2} \sum_{y=0}^{3} e^{2\pi i xy / 4} a_y |y\rangle$

This transformation **spreads the amplitude across multiple basis states**, enabling **parallel computation of multiple frequency components**.

---

4. Applications of the QFT

The QFT is a critical tool in many quantum algorithms, including:

Shor's Algorithm (Prime Factorization)

- The **QFT is used to efficiently factor large numbers**, solving a problem that would take **classical computers millions of years**.
- This has major implications for **cryptography**, potentially breaking RSA encryption.

Quantum AI and Machine Learning

- The QFT is used to **accelerate AI models**, enabling **fast transformations between data representations**.
- **Quantum convolutional networks** leverage QFT for feature extraction in **computer vision**.

Signal Processing

- The QFT enhances **speech recognition, image compression, and sound processing** in quantum-enhanced AI systems.

Table: Mathematical Comparison - Classical vs. Quantum Computing

Feature	Classical Computing	Quantum Computing
Data Representation	Bits (0 or 1)	Qubits (superposition: 0 and 1)
State Space	Linear increase in complexity	Exponential increase with qubit count
Operations	Boolean logic (AND, OR, XOR)	Quantum logic (unitary matrices)
Algorithm Complexity	Scales polynomially or exponentially	Can scale logarithmically for certain problems
Superposition	Not possible	Qubits exist in multiple states simultaneously
Entanglement	No direct equivalent	Enables instant correlations between qubits
Parallelism	Limited (multi-core processing)	Quantum parallelism processes all states at once
Error Handling	Redundancy and error correction codes	Quantum error correction needed for stability

Factorization Speed	Takes exponential time	Polynomial time (Shor's Algorithm)
Fourier Transform	Discrete Fourier Transform (DFT)	Quantum Fourier Transform (QFT), exponentially faster
Machine Learning Training	Data-intensive, computationally expensive	QML optimizes model training via quantum speedup
Optimization Algorithms	Simulated annealing, gradient descent	Quantum annealing, Grover's search

This section covered the **mathematical foundations essential for Quantum Machine Learning**, including:

1. **Tensor Notation** for handling multi-qubit systems.
2. **The Quantum Fourier Transform (QFT)** and its applications in AI.
3. **A mathematical comparison of classical vs. quantum computing**, highlighting quantum's superiority in **speed, parallelism, and AI performance**.

The next sections will explore **Quantum Neural Networks and Practical Applications of Quantum AI**, further bridging quantum computing with artificial intelligence.

Chapter 4

What is Quantum Machine Learning (QML)?

Quantum Machine Learning (QML) is a rapidly emerging field that combines **quantum computing** and **artificial intelligence (AI)** to unlock new computational capabilities. As AI models become more complex, they demand increasingly **powerful computing resources**. Traditional computing, even with **advanced GPUs and TPUs**, struggles to handle the exponential growth of data and computational complexity.

Quantum computing, with its ability to **process vast amounts of information simultaneously**, offers a promising alternative to classical AI techniques. This chapter explores **how quantum computing intersects with AI, the key differences between classical machine learning and quantum machine learning, and the transformative potential of QML for the future of artificial intelligence**.

The Intersection of AI and Quantum Computing

1. The Need for Quantum Computing in AI

Artificial Intelligence has witnessed **remarkable progress** in recent years, with breakthroughs in **deep learning, reinforcement learning, and generative AI**. However, classical AI models face significant computational limitations, such as:

- **High computational costs** for training deep learning models.
- **Exponential growth in data requirements**, making it difficult to scale AI.

- **Limited optimization efficiency**, particularly in areas like reinforcement learning and combinatorial problems.

Quantum computing introduces **a fundamentally new approach** to computation that could overcome these limitations.

How Quantum Computing Enhances AI

Quantum computing enhances AI by:

1. **Providing Quantum Parallelism:** Quantum computers can **process multiple AI models simultaneously** using **superposition and entanglement**, drastically reducing training time.
2. **Improving Optimization Algorithms:** Quantum-based search and optimization techniques like **Grover's Algorithm** improve machine learning model efficiency.
3. **Handling High-Dimensional Data:** Quantum computing can **process and extract features from extremely high-dimensional data**, which is difficult for classical AI models.
4. **Accelerating Neural Network Training:** Quantum circuits can replace certain classical AI components, significantly **reducing the number of operations required to train deep learning models**.

---

2. Quantum Machine Learning (QML): A New Computational Paradigm

Quantum Machine Learning (QML) applies **quantum computing principles** to **AI and machine learning algorithms**. By leveraging **quantum bits (qubits), quantum superposition, and entanglement**, QML enables machine learning models to **explore solutions more efficiently than classical AI models**.

How QML Works

QML works by applying **quantum-enhanced data processing techniques** to classical ML tasks such as:

- **Pattern Recognition:** Quantum models process large datasets faster.
- **Feature Mapping:** Quantum kernels improve feature extraction for AI models.

- **Reinforcement Learning:** Quantum states enhance decision-making in AI systems.

The **core advantage of QML** lies in its ability to process **massive parallel computations** using qubits, while classical AI models rely on **sequential computation using bits**.

Key Differences Between Classical ML and Quantum ML

The key distinction between **Classical Machine Learning (ML)** and **Quantum Machine Learning (QML)** lies in **how they process, store, and manipulate data**. While classical ML models operate within the limitations of **classical computing**, QML harnesses **quantum mechanics to enhance learning capabilities**.

1. Fundamental Computational Approach

Feature	Classical Machine Learning (ML)	Quantum Machine Learning (QML)
Computation Type	Uses classical bits (0s and 1s)	Uses quantum bits (qubits) with superposition
Information Storage	Explicit data storage in memory	Quantum states encode multiple data points simultaneously
Algorithm Complexity	Scales linearly or exponentially	Can achieve exponential speedup for certain tasks
Optimization Speed	Requires extensive computation time	Quantum optimization techniques (e.g., Grover's Algorithm) accelerate training
Data Processing	Relies on feature selection and dimensionality reduction	Uses quantum feature mapping for high-dimensional data

Training Time	Increases with model complexity	Can reduce training time using quantum parallelism

2. Machine Learning Model Architecture

Feature	Classical ML	Quantum ML
Neural Networks	Uses fully connected layers	Quantum neural networks (QNNs) use quantum circuits
Feature Extraction	Requires preprocessing (PCA, t-SNE)	Quantum-enhanced feature selection improves efficiency
Gradient Descent	Uses backpropagation	Quantum gradient descent accelerates training
Error Handling	Requires large labeled datasets for generalization	Quantum noise and entanglement introduce new challenges

Example: In classical ML, a neural network **must iteratively adjust weights** to minimize loss. Quantum ML **updates multiple parameters simultaneously**, making learning faster.

3. Data Representation in Classical vs. Quantum ML

One of the most **significant differences** between classical and quantum ML is **how data is represented and processed**.

Classical Machine Learning Data Representation

- Classical ML represents data as **vectors** in a finite-dimensional space.
- Data preprocessing techniques such as **principal component analysis (PCA)** or **dimensionality reduction** are needed to handle large datasets.
- Classical models often struggle with **high-dimensional and complex datasets**.

Quantum Machine Learning Data Representation

- QML represents data using **quantum states** in a **high-dimensional Hilbert space**.
- Quantum encoding techniques **map classical data into a quantum system**, reducing preprocessing overhead.
- Quantum kernels allow for **efficient classification and clustering** of large datasets.

Example: Classical support vector machines (SVMs) require a kernel function to process **non-linearly separable data**. Quantum-enhanced SVMs leverage **quantum kernels** to classify data more efficiently.

---

4. Computational Speed and Efficiency

Quantum ML provides **significant speedup** over classical ML models in various applications:

Task	Classical ML Time Complexity	Quantum ML Time Complexity
Search Algorithms	$O(N)$	$O(\sqrt{N})$ (Grover's Algorithm)
Factorization	Exponential	Polynomial (Shor's Algorithm)
Feature Selection	$O(2^n)$ (Exponential)	$O(n^2)$ (Polynomial)
Quantum Kernels in ML	Requires large computation resources	Reduces dimensionality overhead

---

5. Use Cases of Classical ML vs. Quantum ML

Application	Classical ML	Quantum ML

Image Recognition	Uses convolutional neural networks (CNNs)	Uses quantum CNNs with faster feature extraction
Natural Language Processing (NLP)	Requires massive labeled datasets	Quantum-enhanced NLP reduces data dependency
Fraud Detection	Relies on big data analytics	Quantum AI detects fraud in real time using quantum search
Optimization (Logistics, Finance)	Uses classical solvers (Simulated Annealing)	Quantum annealing finds optimal solutions exponentially faster

Example:

- **AI in Finance:** Classical ML models require **Monte Carlo simulations** for risk assessment, taking **hours or days**.
- **Quantum AI models** process **multiple risk factors simultaneously**, reducing calculation time to **minutes or seconds**.

The Future of Quantum Machine Learning

As **quantum hardware advances**, QML is expected to revolutionize AI research. While classical ML will continue to dominate in everyday applications, **quantum-enhanced ML will play a critical role in high-performance computing tasks** such as:

- **Drug discovery and molecular simulation**
- **Cryptography and secure communication**
- **Real-time data analytics and financial modeling**
- **AI-driven robotics and automation**

With companies like **Google, IBM, and Microsoft investing heavily in quantum AI**, the future of machine learning is shifting towards **quantum-enhanced intelligence**.

Quantum Machine Learning is redefining **how AI models are trained, optimized, and executed**. By leveraging **quantum mechanics**, QML enables AI models to **process information exponentially faster than classical methods**.

Potential Benefits and Challenges of Quantum Machine Learning (QML)

Quantum Machine Learning (QML) represents a **paradigm shift** in the way artificial intelligence processes information. By leveraging the principles of **quantum computing**, QML has the potential to **accelerate computations, optimize complex systems, and enhance AI capabilities** beyond what classical methods can achieve. However, despite its promise, QML also faces **significant challenges**, including hardware limitations, noise sensitivity, and algorithmic constraints.

This section explores the **key benefits** of QML and the **challenges that must be overcome** for widespread adoption.

1. Potential Benefits of Quantum Machine Learning

1.1. Exponential Speedup in AI Model Training

One of the most significant advantages of QML is its ability to **train AI models faster** than classical methods. Traditional machine learning models, especially deep learning networks, require **massive amounts of data and computational power**. Quantum computing offers:

- **Quantum Parallelism** – Quantum superposition allows AI models to process **multiple states simultaneously**, drastically reducing training time.
- **Faster Gradient Descent** – Quantum optimization techniques can improve AI training efficiency by reducing the number of required iterations.

Example:
 In classical machine learning, training a deep learning model like **GPT-4** requires

thousands of GPUs running for weeks. With **quantum-enhanced AI**, training could be completed **in a fraction of the time**.

1.2. Improved Optimization for Complex Problems

Many AI applications, such as **supply chain management, financial modeling, and drug discovery**, involve solving **complex optimization problems**. QML introduces **quantum algorithms** that outperform classical optimization methods:

- **Grover's Algorithm** speeds up AI search and optimization tasks from **O(N) to O($\sqrt{N}$)**.
- **Quantum Annealing** finds optimal solutions for **combinatorial optimization problems** faster than classical methods.

Example:

- Classical AI struggles with **protein folding simulations** in medical research, which take weeks to compute.
- **Quantum AI can simulate protein interactions in minutes**, accelerating drug discovery.

1.3. Enhanced Feature Extraction and Data Encoding

Quantum computing provides **new techniques for encoding and processing data**, enabling:

- **Quantum Feature Mapping** – Transforms complex, high-dimensional data into **quantum feature spaces** for more efficient learning.
- **Quantum Kernels** – Enhance support vector machines (SVMs) and other ML models by capturing **nonlinear patterns** more effectively.

Example:

- Classical AI struggles with **high-dimensional NLP tasks**, requiring large datasets.
- **Quantum NLP techniques** use **quantum embeddings** to process language faster with fewer resources.

41

1.4. Quantum AI for Secure Cryptography and Cybersecurity

Quantum computing offers **stronger security mechanisms** for AI-based encryption and **fraud detection systems**:

- **Quantum Cryptography** secures AI models against cyber threats using **Quantum Key Distribution (QKD)**.
- **Quantum Secure AI** prevents hacking of AI-driven financial systems and sensitive government data.

Example:

- Traditional AI-based encryption methods like RSA are **vulnerable to quantum attacks**.
- **Quantum AI can implement post-quantum cryptographic techniques** to protect sensitive information.

1.5. Quantum-Powered AI in Big Data Analytics

Quantum computing **enhances AI's ability to process large-scale datasets** in fields like:

- **Financial markets (real-time risk assessment)**
- **Climate modeling and environmental predictions**
- **AI-driven recommendation systems (e.g., Netflix, Amazon, Spotify)**

By **processing multiple data points in parallel**, QML can improve real-time **decision-making and predictive modeling**.

---

2. Challenges of Quantum Machine Learning

Despite its promise, QML is still in its early stages, facing several challenges that must be addressed before it can be widely adopted.

2.1. Hardware Limitations and Scalability Issues

- **Current quantum hardware is highly experimental**, with only a limited number of stable qubits available.

- **Noise and decoherence** affect quantum computations, making it difficult to scale QML algorithms.
- **Quantum error correction** is necessary, but current methods introduce computational overhead.

Example:

- Google's **Sycamore processor** demonstrated **quantum supremacy**, but current quantum chips still struggle with **scalability and reliability**.

2.2. Algorithmic Complexity and Lack of Standardization

- **QML algorithms are still in development**, with limited practical implementations.
- Many **quantum AI frameworks** (Qiskit, Cirq, PennyLane) are in their infancy, requiring **custom quantum coding expertise**.
- There is **no universal standard for quantum deep learning architectures**, making adoption difficult for industries.

Example:

- While classical AI frameworks like **TensorFlow and PyTorch** have standardized deep learning models, **QML lacks mature tools and libraries**.

2.3. High Cost of Quantum Computing Infrastructure

- **Quantum computers require cryogenic cooling (near absolute zero)**, making them expensive to operate.
- **Access to quantum hardware is limited**, with cloud-based quantum computing services being costly.

Example:

- Classical AI models can be trained on **consumer GPUs**, while **QML requires specialized quantum processors (QPU)**, which are not widely available.

2.4. Lack of Quantum AI Talent and Expertise

43

- **Quantum computing and AI are highly specialized fields**, requiring expertise in **linear algebra, quantum mechanics, and machine learning**.
- There is a **shortage of quantum AI researchers and engineers**, slowing down industry adoption.

Example:

- AI developers trained in **deep learning** need **additional quantum computing knowledge** to work on QML projects.

2.5. Noise and Quantum Error Correction Challenges

- Quantum systems are highly **sensitive to external disturbances** (electromagnetic interference, temperature fluctuations).
- **Quantum noise leads to errors**, making it difficult to train stable AI models.

Example:

- While classical AI models can be fine-tuned using **gradient descent**, quantum models suffer from **noise-related inaccuracies** that are difficult to correct.

Flowchart: How Quantum Machine Learning Works

Below is a step-by-step flowchart illustrating **how QML processes and enhances AI models**:

plaintext
CopyEdit

```
Start
  |
  |---> Classical Data Input
  |        (Images, Text, Sensor Data)
  |
  |---> Quantum Encoding
  |        (Quantum Feature Mapping)
```

```
|
|---> Apply Quantum Algorithms
|        (Quantum Kernels, Quantum Neural Networks)
|
|---> Quantum Training and Optimization
|        (Quantum Gradient Descent, Quantum Grover's Search)
|
|---> Quantum Computation
|        (Superposition, Entanglement, Quantum Parallelism)
|
|---> Measurement and Output
|        (Convert Quantum Results to Classical Data)
|
|---> Classical Post-Processing
|        (AI Model Interpretation, Visualization)
|
End
```

Key Stages Explained

1. **Classical Data Input** – Traditional AI datasets (e.g., images, text) are fed into the QML pipeline.
2. **Quantum Encoding** – Data is transformed into **quantum feature representations** using quantum circuits.
3. **Quantum Algorithms** – Quantum kernels or quantum-enhanced deep learning architectures process the data.
4. **Quantum Training & Optimization** – AI models leverage quantum gradient descent and Grover's search for fast learning.
5. **Quantum Computation** – Qubits process data in **parallel** using quantum operations.
6. **Measurement & Output** – The quantum state is measured, and results are **converted into classical data**.
7. **Classical Post-Processing** – AI models interpret quantum results and produce final predictions.

Quantum Machine Learning presents **game-changing benefits** in AI, including **faster training, improved optimization, quantum-enhanced feature extraction, and advanced security applications**. However, **hardware limitations, cost, and algorithmic complexity** remain major hurdles for widespread adoption.

As **quantum computing technology matures**, QML will become a **critical tool for solving AI challenges that classical computing cannot handle**. The next sections will explore **Quantum Data Representation, Quantum Neural Networks, and Real-World Applications of QML**, further bridging the gap between **AI and quantum computing**.

Chapter 5

Quantum Data Representation in AI

Quantum Machine Learning (QML) relies on the **efficient representation of data in quantum systems**. Unlike classical AI, which processes data as **vectors in finite-dimensional spaces**, quantum AI encodes information using **qubits, superposition, and entanglement**. Properly encoding classical data into quantum states is **crucial for leveraging quantum computing advantages** in artificial intelligence.

This chapter explores **Quantum Encoding Techniques and Quantum Feature Mapping**, which form the foundation for **quantum-enhanced AI models**.

Quantum Encoding Techniques

1. The Need for Quantum Encoding

Before classical data can be processed by a **quantum machine learning model**, it must be **encoded** into quantum states. This process is called **quantum data representation** and is a key component of **Quantum AI workflows**.

Challenges of Classical Data Representation in AI:

- **High Dimensionality:** Classical AI struggles with large-scale data that grows exponentially in complexity.
- **Feature Extraction Limitations:** Traditional feature engineering methods require **manual optimization**.
- **Computational Bottlenecks:** Classical AI models are limited by **CPU and GPU processing constraints**.

Quantum encoding techniques **map classical data into quantum states**, enabling **faster processing and improved feature selection**.

---

2. Types of Quantum Encoding Techniques

Several encoding methods exist for converting classical data into **quantum states**. The choice of encoding technique depends on the **AI model requirements** and the type of data being processed.

2.1. Basis Encoding (Computational Basis Representation)

Concept:

- Classical bits **xxx** are directly mapped to quantum basis states $|x\rangle|x\rangle|x\rangle$.
- This is the **simplest** quantum encoding technique, but **lacks efficiency for complex AI models**.

Example:
A binary string **x=101x = 101x=101** is encoded as:

$$|x\rangle=|101\rangle| x \rangle = | 101 \rangle|x\rangle=|101\rangle$$

Use Case:

- **Quantum logic operations** where binary state representation is required.

2.2. Amplitude Encoding (Efficient Quantum Representation)

Concept:

- Classical data is stored in the **amplitude coefficients** of quantum states.
- This allows encoding **high-dimensional data** into **a small number of qubits**.

Example:
A normalized classical data vector **[a0,a1,a2,a3][a_0, a_1, a_2, a_3][a0,a1,a2,a3]** is encoded as:

$$|\psi\rangle=a0|00\rangle+a1|01\rangle+a2|10\rangle+a3|11\rangle| \psi \rangle = a_0 | 00 \rangle + a_1 | 01 \rangle + a_2 | 10 \rangle + a_3 | 11 \rangle|\psi\rangle=a0|00\rangle+a1|01\rangle+a2|10\rangle+a3|11\rangle$$

Advantages:

48

- **Highly efficient representation**, requiring only **logarithmic qubits**.
- Enables **fast computation of distances in AI models**.

Use Case:

- **Quantum Support Vector Machines (QSVMs)** for high-dimensional classification tasks.

2.3. Angle Encoding (Quantum Feature Embedding)

Concept:

- Classical data values are encoded as **rotational angles of qubits**.
- A classical feature **xxx** is mapped using the **rotation operator**:

$Rx(x)=\cos(x)|0\rangle+\sin(x)|1\rangle R\_x(x) = \cos(x) |0\rangle + \sin(x) |1\rangle Rx(x)=\cos(x)|0\rangle+\sin(x)|1\rangle$

Example:
For a classical feature vector **[x1,x2][x_1, x_2][x1,x2]**, the quantum-encoded state is:

$|\psi\rangle=Rx(x1)\otimes Rx(x2)|\psi\rangle = R\_x(x\_1) \otimes R\_x(x\_2)|\psi\rangle=Rx(x1)\otimes Rx(x2)$

Advantages:

- **Suitable for deep learning models** requiring non-linear feature mapping.
- **Preserves quantum entanglement**, allowing complex AI correlations.

Use Case:

- **Quantum Neural Networks (QNNs)** for AI-driven speech and image recognition.

2.4. Qubit Encoding (One-Hot Quantum Representation)

Concept:

49

- Each classical data point is represented using **a separate qubit state**.

Example:
A categorical dataset with **four classes** can be encoded as:

|00⟩,|01⟩,|10⟩,|11⟩| 00 \rangle, | 01 \rangle, | 10 \rangle, | 11 \rangle|00⟩,|01⟩,|10⟩,|11⟩

Advantages:

- **Best suited for categorical data in AI models.**
- **Simple to implement but requires more qubits.**

Use Case:

- **Quantum AI models for natural language processing (NLP).**

Quantum Feature Mapping for AI Models

1. What is Quantum Feature Mapping?

Classical AI models often struggle to **separate non-linearly distributed data**. In quantum AI, **Quantum Feature Mapping** transforms classical data into a **higher-dimensional quantum Hilbert space**, allowing **more efficient classification and regression models**.

How It Works:

- A classical input **xxx** is mapped to a **quantum feature state** $|\phi(x)\rangle$|\phi(x)\rangle|ϕ(x)⟩.
- Quantum gates are applied to **enhance non-linear features** of the data.
- The transformed quantum state **improves AI model accuracy**.

Advantages of Quantum Feature Mapping:
Better separation of non-linear data.
Faster computation of kernel functions.
Increased expressiveness for AI models.

---

2. Types of Quantum Feature Mapping

2.1. Quantum Kernel Methods (Quantum Support Vector Machines - QSVMs)

Concept:

- Classical ML models rely on **kernel functions** to separate data in high-dimensional space.
- **Quantum kernels** provide an **exponential advantage** over classical methods.

Mathematical Representation:
A quantum kernel function **K(xi,xj)K(x_i, x_j)K(xi,xj)** is computed as:

K(xi,xj)=|⟨ϕ(xi)|ϕ(xj)⟩|2K(x_i, x_j) = | \langle \phi(x_i) | \phi(x_j) \rangle |^2K(xi,xj)=|⟨ϕ(xi)|ϕ(xj)⟩|2

where |ϕ(xi)⟩|\phi(x_i)\rangle|ϕ(xi)⟩ represents the quantum-mapped data.

Use Case:

- **Quantum-enhanced AI models for fraud detection and medical diagnosis.**

2.2. Variational Quantum Feature Mapping (Hybrid Quantum-Classical AI)

Concept:

- Uses **parameterized quantum circuits (PQCs)** to encode features dynamically.
- The parameters are **trained using gradient descent**, similar to classical deep learning.

Example:
A variational quantum circuit encodes classical features as:

|ψ(x)⟩=U(θ)|0⟩| \psi(x) \rangle = U(\theta) | 0 \rangle|ψ(x)⟩=U(θ)|0⟩

where **U(θ)U(\theta)U(θ)** is a quantum gate parameterized by trainable weights **θ\thetaθ**.

Advantages:

- **Combines quantum and classical AI models** for real-world applications.
- **Enhances AI decision-making using quantum correlations**.

Use Case:

- **Quantum-enhanced deep learning for real-time speech processing and autonomous vehicles**.

Comparison Table: Classical vs. Quantum Data Representation in AI

Feature	Classical Data Representation	Quantum Data Representation
Feature Mapping	Uses hand-crafted kernel functions	Uses quantum-enhanced feature spaces
Dimensionality Reduction	Requires PCA or t-SNE	Quantum embeddings naturally reduce dimensions
Computational Efficiency	Slower with large datasets	Processes exponentially larger datasets
Kernel Computation	Requires large memory allocation	Uses quantum parallelism for faster computations
Optimization Performance	Slower convergence	Quantum optimization speeds up AI training

Quantum Data Representation is a **critical component** of Quantum Machine Learning, enabling AI models to:

Encode high-dimensional data efficiently
 Leverage quantum feature mapping for better pattern recognition
Process AI computations exponentially faster than classical models

As Quantum AI continues to evolve, **Quantum Feature Mapping and Encoding Techniques** will play a **foundational role in building next-generation AI applications**.

52

The next sections will explore **Quantum Neural Networks, Quantum Deep Learning, and real-world AI applications powered by QML**.

State Preparation for Machine Learning Tasks

1. Understanding Quantum State Preparation in AI

Quantum **state preparation** is the process of encoding classical data into **quantum states** so that it can be processed by **Quantum Machine Learning (QML) models**. The effectiveness of **quantum learning algorithms** largely depends on how efficiently **classical data** is transformed into **a quantum representation**.

Why is State Preparation Important?

- Bridges the gap between classical AI and quantum computing.
- Determines computational efficiency and quantum advantage.
- Affects training time, model accuracy, and scalability in QML.

Since qubits operate under the principles of **superposition and entanglement**, proper state preparation ensures that **quantum AI models can leverage quantum parallelism** to achieve **exponential speedup**.

---

2. Methods of Quantum State Preparation for Machine Learning

There are several approaches to **encoding and preparing quantum states** for machine learning. The choice of state preparation depends on **dataset structure, computational complexity, and AI model requirements**.

2.1. Basis State Encoding (Computational Basis Representation)

Concept:

53

- Each classical data point is **directly mapped to a quantum computational basis state**.
- This method is simple but **inefficient for high-dimensional datasets**.

Example:
A classical binary dataset containing **four samples**:

{00,01,10,11}\{ 00, 01, 10, 11 \}{00,01,10,11}

is **mapped to**:

$|00\rangle, |01\rangle, |10\rangle, |11\rangle$|00\rangle, |01\rangle, |10\rangle, |11\rangle$|00\rangle, |01\rangle, |10\rangle, |11\rangle$

Advantages:
Simple to implement.
Useful for **categorical data representation**.

Limitations:
Not scalable for large datasets.
Cannot leverage **quantum superposition** for parallelism.

Use Case:

- **Quantum Boolean logic operations in AI models.**

2.2. Amplitude Encoding (High-Dimensional Data Representation)

Concept:

- Classical data is **encoded into the probability amplitudes of quantum states**.
- This method is highly **efficient** for handling **large datasets** with fewer qubits.

Example:
A classical feature vector $x=[x_0,x_1,x_2,x_3]$x = [x_0, x_1, x_2, x_3]$x=[x0,x1,x2,x3]$ is normalized and encoded as:

$|\psi\rangle = x_0|00\rangle + x_1|01\rangle + x_2|10\rangle + x_3|11\rangle$ \psi \rangle = x_0 |00\rangle + x_1 |01\rangle + x_2 |10\rangle + x_3 |11\rangle$|\psi\rangle=x_0|00\rangle+x_1|01\rangle+x_2|10\rangle+x_3|11\rangle$

Advantages:
 Efficient for **high-dimensional feature encoding**.
 Requires **logarithmically fewer qubits** than basis encoding.

Limitations:
 Requires **quantum normalization**.
 Difficult to implement on current quantum hardware.

Use Case:

- **Quantum deep learning models that process high-dimensional images and time-series data.**

2.3. Angle Encoding (Quantum Feature Space Mapping)

Concept:

- Classical features are encoded into **quantum rotational angles**.
- Uses **rotation gates** (RxR_xRx, RyR_yRy, RzR_zRz) to transform data into **quantum circuit form**.

Example:
 A classical data point **xxx** is encoded as:

$$|\psi\rangle = R_x(x)|0\rangle + R_y(x)|1\rangle$$ | \psi \rangle = R_x(x) |0\rangle + R_y(x) |1\rangle |ψ⟩=Rx(x)|0⟩+Ry(x)|1⟩

where:

$$R_x(x) = \cos(x)|0\rangle + \sin(x)|1\rangle$$ R_x(x) = \cos(x) |0\rangle + \sin(x) |1\rangle Rx(x)=cos(x)|0⟩+sin(x)|1⟩

Advantages:
 Best for non-linear feature transformation.
 Preserves entanglement, allowing **better AI decision-making**.

Limitations:
 Limited expressiveness for large datasets.
 Requires additional quantum **entanglement gates** for complex AI tasks.

Use Case:

- **Quantum Neural Networks (QNNs) in AI image classification and pattern recognition.**

2.4. Quantum Circuit-Based Encoding (Variational Quantum Circuits - VQC)

Concept:

- Uses **parameterized quantum circuits (PQCs)** for dynamic feature encoding.
- **Quantum gates are trained like deep learning parameters**, improving AI adaptability.

Example:
A **quantum-enhanced deep learning model** encodes data as:

$$|ψ(x)⟩=U(θ)|0⟩| \psi(x) \rangle = U(\theta) | 0 \rangle | ψ(x)⟩=U(θ)|0⟩$$

where **U(θ)U(\theta)U(θ)** is a trainable **quantum circuit unitary operation**.

Advantages:
Combines classical deep learning with quantum computing.
Allows AI models to dynamically adjust feature representations.

Limitations:
Requires a **hybrid quantum-classical framework (Qiskit, PennyLane, Cirq)**.
Needs high-fidelity quantum processors for training large models.

Use Case:

- Quantum-enhanced deep learning models for AI-driven speech recognition and medical diagnosis.

3. Practical Implementation of Quantum State Preparation

3.1. Quantum AI Workflow Using State Preparation
plaintext
CopyEdit
Start

```
|
|---> Classical Data Input
|       (e.g., Images, Text, Financial Data)
|
|---> Quantum State Preparation
|       (Basis Encoding, Amplitude Encoding, Angle Encoding)
|
|---> Quantum Machine Learning Model
|       (Quantum Kernels, Quantum Neural Networks)
|
|---> Measurement and Output
|       (Convert Quantum Results to Classical Data)
|
|---> AI Model Optimization
|       (Quantum Gradient Descent, Hybrid AI Training)
|
End
```

Table: Classical vs. Quantum Data Representation Methods

Feature	Classical Data Representation	Quantum Data Representation
Encoding Mechanism	Uses numerical vectors	Uses quantum superposition, amplitudes, or angles
Dimensionality Handling	Requires dimensionality reduction (PCA, t-SNE)	Encodes high-dimensional data into **logarithmically fewer qubits**

Feature Mapping	Manually engineered features	Quantum kernels automatically enhance feature separation
Computation Speed	Limited by classical processors	Uses quantum parallelism for **exponential speedup**
Kernel Computation	Slow for non-linear problems	Quantum kernels execute exponentially faster
Scalability	Requires large storage and processing power	Reduces data footprint via quantum encoding
Optimization Complexity	Gradient-based learning	Uses quantum gradient descent for efficient learning

State preparation is a **critical step in Quantum Machine Learning**, ensuring that AI models **leverage quantum principles effectively**. Proper encoding techniques allow **AI models to process complex data with greater speed, efficiency, and accuracy** than classical methods.

Key Takeaways:
   Quantum Encoding Techniques (Basis Encoding, Amplitude Encoding, Angle Encoding, Variational Circuits) enhance AI data processing.
   Quantum Feature Mapping improves non-linear classification and regression models.
   Quantum AI outperforms classical models in handling high-dimensional datasets.

As Quantum AI advances, **state preparation will become a fundamental aspect of building next-generation AI applications**. The next sections will explore **Quantum Neural Networks, Quantum Deep Learning, and Real-World AI Applications of QML**.

State Preparation for Machine Learning Tasks

1. Introduction to Quantum State Preparation in Machine Learning

Quantum Machine Learning (QML) aims to leverage quantum computing's **superposition, entanglement, and parallelism** to enhance AI models. However, for classical data to be processed within a quantum system, it must be **efficiently prepared and encoded into quantum states**.

Quantum **state preparation** is one of the most critical steps in QML, as improper encoding can lead to **loss of quantum advantage**, increasing computational complexity rather than reducing it. This section explores **state preparation methods, their role in AI models, and how they compare to classical data representation techniques**.

---

2. Why is State Preparation Important in QML?

Unlike classical AI, where data is stored as **numerical feature vectors** in memory, quantum AI processes information through **qubits, quantum gates, and quantum measurements**. The way data is prepared impacts:

- **How efficiently the AI model learns patterns.**
- **The ability to handle large-scale datasets in a quantum framework.**
- **The computational resources required to run the quantum AI model.**

The choice of state preparation method depends on the **data type, problem complexity, and available quantum hardware**.

---

3. Methods of Quantum State Preparation for AI Models

3.1. Basis State Encoding (Computational Basis Representation)

Concept:

- This is the **simplest encoding method**, where classical binary data is directly mapped to computational basis states $|0\rangle$ and $|1\rangle$.
- Each classical bit $x \in \{0,1\}$ is converted into a corresponding qubit state.

Example:
For a **binary dataset** containing the numbers **00, 01, 10, and 11**, the quantum representation is:

$$|00\rangle, |01\rangle, |10\rangle, |11\rangle$$

Advantages:
Simple to implement and requires minimal quantum operations.
Works well for classical Boolean logic-based AI models.

Limitations:
Inefficient for high-dimensional datasets.
Does not take advantage of quantum superposition or entanglement.

Use Case:

- **Quantum Boolean AI models** where data follows a strict binary structure.

3.2. Amplitude Encoding (Efficient High-Dimensional Representation)

Concept:

- Instead of mapping data to basis states, **classical feature values are embedded into quantum probability amplitudes**.
- This technique allows **large feature vectors to be encoded into a small number of qubits**, reducing memory requirements.

Example:
A classical data vector $x = [x_0, x_1, x_2, x_3]$ is normalized and encoded as:

60

$|ψ⟩=x0|00⟩+x1|01⟩+x2|10⟩+x3|11⟩|$ \psi \rangle = x_0 |00\rangle + x_1 |01\rangle + x_2 |10\rangle + x_3 |11\rangle $|ψ⟩=x0|00⟩+x1|01⟩+x2|10⟩+x3|11⟩$

Advantages:
 Highly efficient for representing complex, high-dimensional datasets.
 Uses fewer qubits to store more data.

Limitations:
 Difficult to implement on current quantum hardware.
 Requires quantum normalization techniques.

Use Case:

- **Quantum-enhanced AI for high-dimensional pattern recognition** (e.g., finance, healthcare).

3.3. Angle Encoding (Quantum Feature Rotation Representation)

Concept:

- Classical features are encoded as **rotational angles of qubits** in quantum space.
- Uses quantum rotation gates **Rx,Ry,RzR_x, R_y, R_zRx,Ry,Rz** to transform feature values into **quantum circuit form**.

Example:
 A classical feature **xxx** is mapped using a quantum rotation:

$|ψ⟩=Rx(x)|0⟩+Ry(x)|1⟩|$ \psi \rangle = R_x(x) |0\rangle + R_y(x) |1\rangle $|1\rangle|ψ⟩=Rx(x)|0⟩+Ry(x)|1⟩$

where:

$Rx(x)=cos(x)|0⟩+sin(x)|1⟩R_x(x) = \cos(x) |0\rangle + \sin(x)|1\rangle Rx(x)=cos(x)|0⟩+sin(x)|1⟩$

Advantages:
 Best suited for non-linear data transformations.
 Works well with quantum neural networks (QNNs).

Limitations:
Limited expressiveness for large datasets.
Additional entanglement gates are required for complex AI tasks.

Use Case:

- Quantum deep learning models in image classification and speech recognition.

3.4. Quantum Circuit-Based Encoding (Variational Quantum Circuits - VQC)

Concept:

- Uses **parameterized quantum circuits (PQCs)** where quantum gates are trained similar to deep learning parameters.
- This allows the **quantum circuit to dynamically adjust** based on AI model requirements.

Example:
A **quantum-enhanced AI model** encodes data as:

$|\psi(x)\rangle = U(\theta)|0\rangle$ | \psi(x) \rangle = U(\theta) | 0 \rangle $|\psi(x)\rangle = U(\theta)|0\rangle$

where $U(\theta)$U(\theta)$U(\theta)$ is a trainable quantum unitary operation.

Advantages:
Combines classical deep learning with quantum processing.
Can dynamically optimize feature representations.

Limitations:
Requires hybrid quantum-classical AI frameworks (Qiskit, PennyLane, Cirq).
Needs access to high-fidelity quantum processors.

Use Case:

62

- Quantum-powered AI models for real-time fraud detection and self-driving cars.

---

4. Practical Implementation of Quantum State Preparation in AI

4.1. Workflow for Quantum AI State Preparation

plaintext
CopyEdit

```
Start
  |
  |---> Classical Data Input
  |        (e.g., Images, Text, Financial Data)
  |
  |---> Quantum State Preparation
  |        (Basis Encoding, Amplitude Encoding, Angle Encoding)
  |
  |---> Quantum Machine Learning Model
  |        (Quantum Kernels, Quantum Neural Networks)
  |
  |---> Measurement and Output
  |        (Convert Quantum Results to Classical Data)
  |
  |---> AI Model Optimization
  |        (Quantum Gradient Descent, Hybrid AI Training)
  |
End
```

This workflow **demonstrates how classical data is transformed into quantum states**, processed by **Quantum AI models**, and finally converted back into meaningful AI predictions.

Table: Classical vs. Quantum Data Representation Methods

Feature	Classical Data Representation	Quantum Data Representation
Encoding Mechanism	Uses numerical vectors and feature engineering	Uses quantum superposition, amplitudes, or angles
Dimensionality Handling	Requires PCA, t-SNE, or feature selection	Encodes high-dimensional data into **logarithmically fewer qubits**
Feature Mapping	Manually designed or precomputed kernels	Quantum kernels **automatically capture complex relationships**
Computation Speed	Limited by classical CPU/GPU processing	Uses quantum parallelism for **exponential speedup**
Kernel Computation	Expensive for non-linear problems	Quantum kernels execute exponentially faster
Scalability	Requires increasing memory and processing power	**Encodes massive datasets with fewer resources**
Optimization Complexity	Uses classical gradient-based learning	Uses **quantum-enhanced gradient descent for faster training**

Quantum **state preparation** is an essential step in **Quantum Machine Learning (QML)**. By transforming classical data into **quantum-encoded states**, AI models can leverage **quantum superposition, entanglement, and parallel computation** to unlock **unprecedented computational efficiency**.

Key Takeaways:

   Quantum Encoding Techniques (Basis Encoding, Amplitude Encoding, Angle Encoding, Variational Circuits) define how data is processed in QML.

   Quantum Feature Mapping enhances **classification and regression tasks** beyond classical AI capabilities.

   Quantum AI outperforms classical AI in handling high-dimensional datasets with fewer computational resources.

As quantum hardware matures, **state preparation techniques will continue to evolve**, shaping the future of **Quantum Deep Learning, Quantum Neural Networks, and AI-driven Quantum Computing Applications**.

Chapter 6

Quantum Neural Networks (QNNs)

Quantum Neural Networks (QNNs) are **revolutionary AI models** that combine the computational power of **quantum computing** with **deep learning**. Unlike classical neural networks, which rely on **matrix multiplications and activation functions**, QNNs use **quantum circuits, superposition, and entanglement** to process information efficiently.

This chapter explores **Quantum Perceptrons and Variational Quantum Circuits (VQCs)**—the fundamental building blocks of quantum deep learning. Understanding these concepts is essential for developing **next-generation AI applications that leverage quantum computing for enhanced efficiency and performance**.

Introduction to Quantum Perceptrons

1. What is a Quantum Perceptron?

A **Quantum Perceptron** is the **quantum equivalent of a classical artificial neuron**. In classical deep learning, a perceptron performs the following operations:

1. **Takes multiple inputs** (feature values from the dataset).
2. **Applies weights** to these inputs.
3. **Passes the weighted sum through an activation function** (e.g., ReLU, sigmoid).
4. **Outputs a value** for further layers in the neural network.

A Quantum Perceptron follows **a similar process but operates in a quantum computing environment**, where computations use **quantum gates instead of mathematical functions**.

---

2. How Does a Quantum Perceptron Work?

Step 1: Quantum State Preparation

- Classical input data is **encoded into quantum states** using **basis encoding, amplitude encoding, or angle encoding**.
- Each quantum perceptron processes **quantum data instead of numerical vectors**.

Step 2: Quantum Weight Application

- Classical perceptrons use **linear weights** for transformation.
- A Quantum Perceptron applies **quantum gates** (e.g., Hadamard, Pauli-X, Rotation gates) to modify qubit states.

Step 3: Quantum Activation Function

- Classical perceptrons apply **ReLU, sigmoid, or tanh** activation functions to determine neuron output.
- Quantum perceptrons use **quantum phase shifts, rotation gates, or interference effects** to achieve non-linearity.

Step 4: Measurement and Output

- The final qubit states are **measured**, and the classical output is extracted.
- The quantum perceptron's result is **fed into subsequent layers** in a hybrid quantum-classical neural network.

---

3. Mathematical Model of a Quantum Perceptron

In classical deep learning, a perceptron computes:

$$y=f(\sum w_i x_i + b) \quad y = f\left(\sum w_i x_i + b \right) \quad y=f(\sum w_i x_i + b)$$

where:

- $x_i x\_i x_i$ are input features.
- $w_i w\_i w_i$ are weights.
- bbb is the bias term.
- $f(x)f(x)f(x)$ is an activation function.

In a Quantum Perceptron, the equivalent computation is:

| ψout)=U(W)|ψin)| \psi_{\text{out}} \rangle = U(W) | \psi_{\text{in}} \rangle |ψout)=U(W)|ψin⟩

where:

- | ψin)| \psi_{\text{in}} \rangle | ψin⟩ is the input quantum state.
- U(W)U(W)U(W) is a quantum gate encoding the weight transformation.
- | ψout)| \psi_{\text{out}} \rangle | ψout⟩ is the output quantum state.

The non-linearity in QNNs is introduced by **quantum entanglement, interference, and measurement**, allowing **highly complex feature transformations**.

---

4. Advantages of Quantum Perceptrons Over Classical Perceptrons

Feature	Classical Perceptron	Quantum Perceptron
Data Encoding	Uses classical numerical vectors	Encodes features as quantum states
Computation Speed	Limited by classical hardware	Uses quantum parallelism for faster processing
Non-Linearity	Achieved via activation functions (ReLU, sigmoid)	Achieved via quantum phase shifts and entanglement
Scalability	Requires **more layers** for complex learning	Handles complex functions with **fewer layers**
Memory Efficiency	Needs **large memory for high-dimensional data**	Stores **exponentially more data using qubits**

Quantum Perceptrons are **more efficient for processing complex datasets**, making them ideal for **quantum-enhanced AI models**.

Variational Quantum Circuits in Deep Learning

1. What are Variational Quantum Circuits (VQCs)?

Variational Quantum Circuits (VQCs) are **quantum analogs of classical deep learning layers**. They are used in **Quantum Neural Networks (QNNs) to process quantum information dynamically**.

VQCs **consist of trainable quantum gates**, similar to how classical deep learning models adjust weights using **gradient descent**. These circuits are optimized using hybrid **quantum-classical learning algorithms**.

2. Structure of a Variational Quantum Circuit (VQC)

A VQC consists of the following **three main components**:

1. Quantum Feature Embedding

- Classical data is **encoded into quantum states** using **angle encoding or amplitude encoding**.
- Feature vectors are **mapped to qubits via rotational quantum gates**.

2. Parameterized Quantum Circuit (PQC) Processing

- Trainable quantum gates **modify qubit states** based on adjustable parameters θ\theta$\theta$.
- Quantum gates act as **learnable weights**, evolving during model training.

3. Quantum Measurement and Output

- The **final qubit states are measured**, extracting results for AI tasks.
- The output is **converted into classical data** for decision-making.

3. Mathematical Model of a Variational Quantum Circuit

The **VQC transformation** on an input state $|\psi_{in}\rangle$| \psi_{\text{in}} \rangle $|\psi_{in}\rangle$ is represented as:

$|\psi_{out}\rangle = U(\theta)|\psi_{in}\rangle$| \psi_{\text{out}} \rangle = U(\theta) | \psi_{\text{in}} \rangle $|\psi_{out}\rangle = U(\theta)|\psi_{in}\rangle$

where:

- $U(\theta)$U(\theta)$U(\theta)$ is a **trainable quantum gate parameterized by θ\theta$\theta$**.
- The parameters θ\theta$\theta$ are updated **using quantum gradient descent**.

The training process follows a **quantum-classical hybrid optimization approach**, where:

1. A **quantum processor** applies $U(\theta)$U(\theta)$U(\theta)$.
2. A **classical optimizer (e.g., Adam, SGD)** updates θ\theta$\theta$.
3. The quantum model iteratively improves **based on measurement feedback**.

---

4. Training a Variational Quantum Circuit (VQC) for Deep Learning

The training loop of a **quantum-enhanced deep learning model** follows:

plaintext
CopyEdit

```
1. Initialize quantum circuit parameters θ randomly
2. Encode classical data into quantum states
3. Apply Variational Quantum Circuit (VQC)
4. Measure qubit states and compute loss function
5. Use a classical optimizer (e.g., Adam) to update θ
6. Repeat until convergence
```

The **quantum-classical hybrid model** leverages the **best of both worlds**:
Quantum efficiency for faster computations
  Classical optimization for stable training

---

5. Applications of Variational Quantum Circuits in AI

VQCs are **widely used in modern AI applications,** including:

Application	Impact of VQCs
Quantum Image Classification	Enhances pattern recognition for quantum deep learning models
Quantum Natural Language Processing (QNLP)	Improves text embeddings for faster AI training
Fraud Detection in Finance	Detects anomalies using quantum-enhanced classification
AI-driven Drug Discovery	Simulates molecular interactions at the quantum level

VQCs **enable deep learning models to scale efficiently,** improving **AI decision-making in complex domains.**

Quantum Neural Networks (QNNs) are transforming AI by introducing **Quantum Perceptrons and Variational Quantum Circuits (VQCs).** These architectures **replace classical deep learning components with quantum circuits,** enabling **exponentially faster computations.**

Quantum Perceptrons leverage entanglement for enhanced learning. Variational Quantum Circuits allow dynamic feature transformations. Quantum AI models outperform classical deep learning in optimization, training speed, and high-dimensional data processing.

As quantum computing advances, **QNNs will become a cornerstone of next-generation AI applications,** accelerating breakthroughs in **computer vision, NLP, and autonomous decision-making.**

Training Quantum Neural Networks: Quantum Gradient Descent

Quantum Neural Networks (QNNs) represent a **new frontier in artificial intelligence**, blending **quantum computing with deep learning**. However, just like classical neural networks require training through **gradient descent**, QNNs also need an optimization mechanism to update **quantum circuit parameters**.

This section covers **Quantum Gradient Descent (QGD)**—a method used to train QNNs by minimizing loss functions and updating quantum gate parameters efficiently.

---

1. The Need for Training in Quantum Neural Networks

In classical deep learning, training involves:

- **Forward propagation:** Inputs pass through layers of the network.
- **Loss computation:** A function calculates how far the predicted output is from the actual value.
- **Backpropagation:** The gradient of the loss is computed and used to adjust weights.

However, in **Quantum Neural Networks (QNNs)**:

- **Quantum circuits replace traditional layers.**
- **Quantum states encode feature data.**
- **Quantum gradient descent optimizes quantum gates.**

Training QNNs efficiently is crucial for **applying quantum deep learning in AI tasks** like **image recognition, NLP, and decision-making**.

---

2. What is Quantum Gradient Descent?

Quantum Gradient Descent (QGD) is the **quantum counterpart of classical gradient descent**. Instead of adjusting numerical weights, QGD **optimizes quantum gate parameters** to minimize an AI model's loss function.

Mathematical Formulation of QGD

In classical neural networks, **gradient descent updates weights using**:

$w_{t+1} = w_t - \eta \frac{\partial L}{\partial w_t}$

where:

- w_t is the weight at step t.
- η is the learning rate.
- L is the loss function.

For **Quantum Neural Networks**, quantum circuits **parameterize gates** as:

$U(\theta) = e^{-i\theta H}$

where:

- θ is the trainable quantum parameter.
- H is a Hamiltonian governing quantum evolution.

The **quantum gradient descent update rule** follows:

$\theta_{t+1} = \theta_t - \eta \frac{\partial L}{\partial \theta_t}$

This equation **adjusts quantum gate parameters** dynamically, improving the quantum AI model's performance.

---

3. The Workflow of Training a QNN with Quantum Gradient Descent

Step 1: Initialize Quantum Parameters

- Randomly assign **initial values to quantum gate parameters** θ\thetaθ.
- Encode input data into **quantum states**.

Step 2: Forward Pass (Quantum Circuit Execution)

- Apply **quantum transformations** on qubits.
- Process input through **Quantum Perceptrons or Variational Quantum Circuits**.

Step 3: Measure Quantum Output

- Measure the final qubit states.
- Convert quantum results to **classical data** for loss computation.

Step 4: Compute Loss Function

- The loss function **quantifies how close the prediction is to the actual value**.
- A common loss function in QML is **Mean Squared Error (MSE)**:

L=1n∑i=1n(yi−y^i)2L = \frac{1}{n} \sum_{i=1}^{n} (y_i - \hat{y}_i)^2L=n1i=1∑n(yi−y^i)2

where yiy_iyi is the actual value and y^i\hat{y}_iy^i is the predicted output.

Step 5: Compute Quantum Gradients

- Use **Quantum Parameter Shift Rules** to calculate derivatives.
- Approximate ∂L∂θ\frac{\partial L}{\partial \theta}∂θ∂L using quantum gates.

Step 6: Update Quantum Parameters

- Apply **Quantum Gradient Descent (QGD)**:

θt+1=θt−η∂L∂θt\theta_{t+1} = \theta_t - \eta \frac{\partial L}{\partial \theta_t}θt+1=θt−η∂θt∂L

- Update the quantum circuit for the next iteration.

Step 7: Repeat Until Convergence

- Continue optimizing quantum parameters **until the loss is minimized**.

4. Methods for Computing Quantum Gradients

Since quantum circuits operate differently from classical deep learning models, **traditional backpropagation does not work**. Instead, QNNs use **Quantum Gradient Approximation Techniques**.

4.1. Parameter Shift Rule (PSR)

- The **most widely used method** for computing quantum gradients.
- Instead of direct differentiation, PSR computes **finite differences in quantum gate parameters**.

Mathematical Formulation: For a quantum function $f(\theta)f(\text{\textbackslash}theta)f(\theta)$, the gradient is computed as:

$$\partial f\partial\theta = f(\theta+\pi 2) - f(\theta-\pi 2)2\frac{\partial f}{\partial \theta} = \frac{f(\theta + \frac{\pi}{2}) - f(\theta - \frac{\pi}{2})}{2}\partial\theta\partial f = 2f(\theta+2\pi) - f(\theta-2\pi)$$

- This **avoids numerical instability** while ensuring **efficient quantum training**.

4.2. Stochastic Quantum Gradient Descent (SQGD)

- Adapts **stochastic optimization** techniques for quantum models.
- Similar to **SGD in classical deep learning**, but applied to quantum circuits.

4.3. Quantum Natural Gradient Descent

- Uses **quantum Fisher information** for more efficient learning.
- More advanced, but provides **higher convergence speed**.

Each method has **advantages and trade-offs**, depending on the **complexity of the quantum AI model**.

Illustration: Quantum Neural Network Architecture

A **Quantum Neural Network (QNN)** follows a layered approach, similar to **classical deep learning models** but with quantum circuits.

Basic QNN Structure:

plaintext

CopyEdit

```
Input Layer (Quantum State Preparation)
  |
  |---> Quantum Perceptron Layer (Qubit Encoding)
  |
  |---> Variational Quantum Circuit (Parameterized Gates)
  |
  |---> Measurement Layer (Extract Quantum Results)
  |
  |---> Classical Post-Processing (Convert to Classical Data)
  |
  Output Layer (AI Prediction)
```

Graphical Representation of a QNN

Below is a visualization of a **Quantum Neural Network (QNN) with Variational Quantum Circuits**:

pgsql
CopyEdit

```
Classical Data Input
          ↓
+----------------------+
| Quantum Data Encoding |
+----------------------+

          ↓
+--------------------------+
| Quantum Perceptron Layer  |
| (Qubits & Parameterized Gates) |
+--------------------------+

          ↓
+--------------------------+
| Variational Quantum Circuit |
| (Trainable Quantum Layers) |
+--------------------------+

          ↓
+-------------------+
```

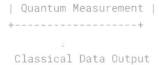

```
| Quantum Measurement |
+--------------------+
          |
  Classical Data Output
```

This **architecture replaces traditional deep learning layers with quantum components**, enhancing computational power.

---

5. Challenges in Training Quantum Neural Networks

Despite their potential, **Quantum Neural Networks (QNNs) face challenges**, including:

Challenge	Impact on Training
Quantum Noise & Decoherence	Quantum gates suffer from **errors due to environmental interference**.
Limited Qubit Availability	Current quantum hardware **supports only a few stable qubits**.
Slow Quantum Gradient Computation	Quantum optimization techniques **require careful parameter tuning**.
Hybrid Quantum-Classical Complexity	**Combining classical AI with quantum circuits** requires specialized algorithms.

To overcome these, researchers are developing **error correction methods, improved qubit stability, and more efficient quantum optimizers**.

6. Future of Quantum Neural Networks and Training Techniques

As quantum technology advances, **Quantum Gradient Descent (QGD)** will become **faster, more efficient, and widely accessible**. Key future developments include:

- **Quantum AI Accelerators** – Specialized hardware for faster QNN training.
- **Advanced Quantum Optimizers** – New algorithms for efficient gradient calculations.
- **Hybrid Quantum-Classical AI Models** – Combining quantum speed with classical deep learning scalability.

These advancements will make **Quantum Deep Learning a game-changer** for AI applications in **finance, healthcare, autonomous systems, and cryptography**.

Quantum Gradient Descent (QGD) is a **breakthrough training technique** that allows Quantum Neural Networks (QNNs) to learn efficiently. By **optimizing quantum gate parameters**, QNNs can **process complex AI tasks exponentially faster than classical models**.

Quantum Perceptrons replace traditional deep learning neurons.
Variational Quantum Circuits (VQCs) enable dynamic quantum feature learning.
Quantum Gradient Descent (QGD) optimizes quantum AI models for real-world applications.

As quantum computing continues to evolve, **Quantum Neural Networks will redefine AI's future**, creating **next-generation deep learning architectures with unprecedented capabilities**.

Chapter 7

Quantum Supervised Learning Models

Quantum Supervised Learning represents a **new paradigm in artificial intelligence**, where classical supervised learning techniques are enhanced using **quantum computing principles**. Traditional supervised learning relies on labeled datasets to train models for **classification and regression tasks**. Quantum Supervised Learning leverages **quantum speedup, entanglement, and parallelism** to **improve accuracy, scalability, and computational efficiency**.

This chapter provides a **comprehensive introduction to supervised learning in Quantum AI** and explores **Quantum Support Vector Machines (QSVMs)**—one of the most powerful quantum-enhanced supervised learning models.

Introduction to Supervised Learning in Quantum AI

1. What is Supervised Learning?

Supervised Learning is a **machine learning paradigm** where an AI model learns from **labeled training data** to make predictions on unseen data. The process involves:

1. **Training Phase**:

    ○ The model learns patterns from **input-output pairs** (X,YX, YX,Y).
    ○ It optimizes a function to **minimize prediction errors**.
2. **Prediction Phase**:

    ○ Once trained, the model generalizes to **new, unseen data**.

Supervised learning is widely used in **image recognition, fraud detection, language translation, and medical diagnosis**.

2. The Need for Quantum Supervised Learning

Classical supervised learning models face **computational bottlenecks**, particularly when handling **high-dimensional data and complex feature spaces**.

Challenges in Classical Supervised Learning

Challenge	Impact
High computational cost	Training deep learning models requires **massive datasets and GPUs**.
Non-linearly separable data	Classical models struggle with **high-dimensional feature spaces**.
Exponential data growth	Handling large-scale datasets **increases training time drastically**.

Quantum computing offers **exponential speedup** for these problems by leveraging **quantum parallelism, quantum feature mapping, and entanglement**.

3. How Quantum Supervised Learning Works

Quantum Supervised Learning enhances classical models by using **quantum state representation, quantum kernels, and quantum optimization algorithms**.

Workflow of Quantum Supervised Learning

```
plaintext
CopyEdit
Start
  |
```

```
|---> Data Encoding into Quantum States
|        (Quantum Feature Mapping)
|
|---> Quantum Model Training
|        (Quantum SVM, Quantum Neural Networks)
|
|---> Quantum Computation
|        (Superposition, Entanglement, Quantum Parallelism)
|
|---> Quantum Measurement
|        (Extract Classical Predictions)
|
|---> AI Model Prediction
|        (Fraud Detection, NLP, Image Classification)
|
End
```

Quantum models **replace traditional learning algorithms** with quantum-enhanced versions such as **Quantum Support Vector Machines (QSVMs), Quantum Neural Networks (QNNs), and Quantum Kernel Methods**.

Quantum Support Vector Machines (QSVM)

Quantum Support Vector Machines (QSVMs) are **quantum-enhanced versions of classical Support Vector Machines (SVMs)**. They use **quantum kernels** to classify high-dimensional data more efficiently than classical SVMs.

---

1. What is a Support Vector Machine (SVM)?

A **Support Vector Machine (SVM)** is a supervised learning algorithm used for **classification and regression**. It works by:

1. Finding the **optimal hyperplane** that separates different classes in a dataset.
2. Maximizing the **margin** between the closest data points (support vectors).
3. Using **kernel tricks** to classify non-linearly separable data.

However, **classical SVMs struggle with high-dimensional data**, making them computationally expensive.

2. How QSVM Improves Classical SVMs

Quantum Support Vector Machines replace **classical kernels with quantum-enhanced feature mappings**, allowing for **exponential speedup** in classification tasks.

Feature	Classical SVM	Quantum SVM (QSVM)
Data Encoding	Uses numerical vectors	Encodes data in **quantum feature space**
Computational Complexity	Increases with dataset size	**Exponential speedup** using quantum kernels
Kernel Trick	Uses **Gaussian, Polynomial, or RBF kernels**	Uses **Quantum Kernel Methods**
Non-Linearity Handling	Requires **computationally expensive feature transformations**	**Encodes non-linear features naturally**
Scalability	Slow for **large-scale classification**	Efficient for **big data processing**

By using **Quantum Kernel Estimation**, QSVMs map **classical data into high-dimensional quantum Hilbert space**, making classification more **efficient and scalable**.

3. How Quantum Kernel Methods Work in QSVM

Quantum Kernel Methods replace **classical kernel functions** (e.g., RBF, polynomial) with **quantum-enhanced feature spaces**.

Mathematical Representation: A classical kernel function is defined as:

$K(xi,xj)=\phi(xi) \cdot \phi(xj)$K(x_i, x_j) = \phi(x_i) \cdot \phi(x_j)$K(xi,xj)=\phi(xi) \cdot \phi(xj)$

where **$\phi(x)$\phi(x)$\phi(x)$** represents the feature transformation.

In Quantum SVM, the **quantum kernel function** is:

$KQ(xi,xj)=|\langle\psi(xi)|\psi(xj)\rangle|^2$K_Q(x_i, x_j) = | \langle \psi(x_i) | \psi(x_j) \rangle |^2$KQ(xi,xj)=|\langle\psi(xi)|\psi(xj)\rangle|^2$

where **$|\psi(x)\rangle|$ \psi(x) \rangle$|\psi(x)\rangle$** is the quantum feature mapping of xxx.

Quantum kernels allow the model to **classify data in exponentially large feature spaces** without explicitly computing them.

---

4. QSVM Training Process

Step 1: Quantum Feature Encoding

- Classical data is transformed into **quantum states** using **amplitude encoding or angle encoding**.

Step 2: Quantum Kernel Computation

- Quantum circuits process data points using **quantum feature maps**.
- The quantum kernel function **$KQ(xi,xj)$K_Q(x_i, x_j)$KQ(xi,xj)$** is computed via quantum gates.

Step 3: Hyperplane Optimization

- The **quantum-enhanced SVM model** finds the optimal hyperplane using **quantum convex optimization**.
- The margin between classes is maximized.

Step 4: Quantum Classification

- Unseen data is passed through the **quantum-trained classifier** for prediction.

---

5. Advantages of QSVM Over Classical SVM

Advantage	Impact on AI Performance
Quantum Speedup	Reduces classification time from $O(N^3)$ to $O(\log N)$
Better Generalization	**Higher accuracy** in classifying non-linear data
Handles Large Datasets	**Scalable to big data problems** (finance, healthcare, cybersecurity)
Exponential Feature Mapping	Transforms data into **high-dimensional quantum space effortlessly**

QSVMs outperform **classical SVMs in complex classification tasks**, particularly in **medical imaging, fraud detection, and quantum-enhanced NLP**.

---

6. Real-World Applications of Quantum Support Vector Machines

Application	How QSVM Enhances AI Models
Financial Fraud Detection	Detects anomalies in large-scale transaction datasets.

Quantum NLP (Natural Language Processing)	Improves text classification and sentiment analysis.
Medical Diagnosis	Classifies disease patterns more efficiently than classical AI models.
Cybersecurity	Enhances threat detection in encrypted datasets.

QSVMs are transforming AI by **enabling faster, more accurate supervised learning models for critical real-world applications**.

Quantum Supervised Learning is **revolutionizing classical AI models** by integrating **quantum feature mapping, quantum kernels, and quantum optimization techniques**. Quantum Support Vector Machines (QSVMs) **outperform classical SVMs** by handling **non-linear classification tasks exponentially faster**.

 Quantum Supervised Learning optimizes AI predictions using quantum kernels.
 QSVMs improve classification accuracy and scalability for high-dimensional data.
 Real-world applications include fraud detection, medical imaging, and cybersecurity.

As quantum computing advances, **QSVMs will play a crucial role in next-generation AI models**, redefining **how AI processes and classifies data**.

The next sections will explore **Quantum Decision Trees, Quantum Deep Learning, and Hybrid Quantum-Classical AI Models**.

Quantum Decision Trees for Classification

Quantum Decision Trees (QDTs) are a **quantum-enhanced alternative** to classical decision trees used for **classification and regression tasks**. Unlike traditional decision trees, which rely on **brute-force feature selection and recursive partitioning**, QDTs leverage **quantum computing principles** such as superposition, entanglement, and quantum parallelism to process large datasets more efficiently.

---

1. What is a Decision Tree in Machine Learning?

A **decision tree** is a **supervised learning algorithm** that structures decisions in a **tree-like model**, where:

- **Internal nodes** represent feature selection questions.
- **Branches** represent decision outcomes.
- **Leaf nodes** represent final classifications or predictions.

Example: A classical decision tree for email spam classification:

plaintext
CopyEdit
```
      Is the email from a known sender?
            /              \
       Yes                No
       /                    \
   Contains "discount"?  Contains "urgent"?
   /          \           /          \
Spam      Not Spam    Spam       Not Spam
```

Classical decision trees operate by **iteratively selecting the best feature** to split the dataset. However, **as the dataset grows, decision trees suffer from exponential complexity**.

---

2. Why Use Quantum Decision Trees?

Classical decision trees require **O(N log N) complexity** to split datasets and find optimal feature separations. **Quantum Decision Trees (QDTs) use quantum parallelism** to **process multiple splits simultaneously,** reducing **training time and improving model efficiency.**

Advantages of Quantum Decision Trees Over Classical Trees

Feature	Classical Decision Trees	Quantum Decision Trees (QDTs)
Computational Speed	O(N log N) complexity	**Exponential speedup** using quantum gates
Feature Selection	Iterative and computationally expensive	Quantum parallelism allows **simultaneous feature selection**
Handling High-Dimension al Data	Struggles with very large datasets	Processes **exponentially large datasets** efficiently
Memory Efficiency	Requires **storing full decision tree**	Stores data as **quantum states** for minimal memory usage
Scalability	Slows down with large datasets	**More scalable** for big data problems

Quantum Decision Trees replace **traditional recursive partitioning with quantum-enhanced feature selection,** leading to **faster and more efficient learning.**

3. How Quantum Decision Trees Work

Step 1: Quantum Feature Encoding

- Classical data points are mapped into **quantum states** using **quantum feature mapping.**
- Feature vectors are **represented as qubits,** allowing for **parallel computation.**

Step 2: Quantum Superposition for Decision Boundaries

- In classical trees, each feature is tested **sequentially**.
- QDTs apply **superposition**, enabling **simultaneous evaluation of multiple features**.

Step 3: Quantum Entanglement for Feature Relationships

- In classical trees, features are **independently analyzed**.
- QDTs use **quantum entanglement to capture feature correlations**, improving classification accuracy.

Step 4: Quantum Measurement for Classification

- After quantum processing, the qubits are **measured**, collapsing the quantum state into **a classification decision**.

---

4. Mathematical Representation of a Quantum Decision Tree

A Quantum Decision Tree can be modeled using **unitary transformations on quantum states**:

$|\psi\rangle = U(\theta)|x\rangle$ | \psi \rangle = U(\theta) | x \rangle $|\psi\rangle=U(\theta)|x\rangle$

where:

- $|x\rangle$ | x \rangle $|x\rangle$ is the quantum-encoded feature vector.
- $U(\theta)$ U(\theta)$U(\theta)$ is a quantum circuit **transforming the input** based on decision thresholds.
- The **final quantum state collapses into a classical classification** through quantum measurement.

This approach allows **exponential speedup** in **decision-making and pattern recognition**.

---

5. Real-World Applications of Quantum Decision Trees

Application	Impact of QDTs
Medical Diagnosis	Classifies diseases more accurately with quantum-enhanced pattern detection.
Fraud Detection	Identifies fraudulent transactions in financial datasets efficiently.
Natural Language Processing (NLP)	Enhances text classification for **sentiment analysis**.
Cybersecurity	Detects cyber threats in real-time using quantum anomaly detection.

Quantum Decision Trees are particularly useful in **high-speed classification tasks**, where classical AI struggles with **scalability and complexity**.

Flowchart: Workflow of Quantum Supervised Learning

Below is a step-by-step **workflow illustrating how Quantum Supervised Learning works** in AI applications:

```
plaintext
CopyEdit
Start
 |
 |---> Classical Data Input
 |        (e.g., Images, Text, Financial Data)
 |
```

```
|---> Quantum Feature Mapping
|        (Basis Encoding, Amplitude Encoding, Angle Encoding)
|
|---> Train Quantum Supervised Learning Model
|        (QSVM, Quantum Decision Tree, Quantum Neural Network)
|
|---> Quantum Computation
|        (Superposition, Entanglement, Quantum Kernel
Optimization)
|
|---> Quantum Measurement
|        (Extract Classical Predictions from Qubits)
|
|---> AI Model Prediction
|        (Spam Detection, Image Classification, Fraud
Detection)
|
End
```

6. Example: Quantum Decision Tree for Spam Classification

Classical Decision Tree for Spam Detection

plaintext
CopyEdit

```
      Is the email from a known sender?
            /              \
       Yes                No
       /                    \
   Contains "discount"?  Contains "urgent"?
    /           \          /          \
Spam       Not Spam    Spam       Not Spam
```

Quantum Decision Tree for Spam Detection

plaintext

90

CopyEdit
```
Quantum Superposition Applied

          |
+---------------------------+
| Quantum Feature Mapping   |
+---------------------------+

          |
+-----------------------------+
| Quantum Decision Tree Branch |
| (Simultaneous Feature Selection) |
+-----------------------------+

          |
+-------------------------+
| Quantum Measurement     |
+-------------------------+

          |
+-----------------------+
| Classification Output |
+-----------------------+
```

This **Quantum Decision Tree processes all features in parallel**, enabling **faster spam classification** than classical decision trees.

Quantum Decision Trees (QDTs) **represent a breakthrough in AI classification models**, offering **faster feature selection, improved scalability, and better handling of high-dimensional datasets**.

Quantum Decision Trees leverage superposition for parallel feature selection. They outperform classical decision trees in high-dimensional classification tasks.
Quantum AI models reduce computational overhead, making big data classification efficient.

As quantum computing technology continues to evolve, **Quantum Decision Trees will play a vital role in the future of AI-driven decision-making**, enabling **more efficient and accurate machine learning models**.

Quantum Decision Trees for Classification

Quantum Decision Trees (QDTs) are the **quantum-enhanced counterpart** of classical decision trees, designed for **classification and regression tasks**. Traditional decision trees follow a **recursive binary split approach** to organize data based on decision rules. However, **as dataset complexity increases, classical decision trees face computational bottlenecks**.

Quantum Decision Trees **leverage quantum computing's superposition and entanglement** to process multiple branches simultaneously, reducing computational time and improving classification accuracy.

---

1. How Decision Trees Work in Machine Learning

A **decision tree** is a **hierarchical model** used for making predictions by **splitting the dataset** based on feature values. It follows a **tree-like structure**:

- **Root Node** → Represents the **entire dataset**.
- **Internal Nodes** → Represent **decision points** (questions).
- **Branches** → Represent possible outcomes.
- **Leaf Nodes** → Represent the **final classification or regression value**.

Example: Classical Decision Tree for Spam Classification

plaintext
CopyEdit
```
      Is the email from a known sender?
            /              \
      Yes                No
      /                      \
  Contains "discount"?  Contains "urgent"?
    /          \          /            \
Spam      Not Spam    Spam        Not Spam
```

Classical decision trees work by **iterating over all features and choosing the best split**, but this process **scales poorly with large datasets**.

---

2. Limitations of Classical Decision Trees

Challenge	Impact
Computational Complexity	Training requires **O(N log N) operations**, making it slow for large datasets.
Overfitting	Classical decision trees often **memorize patterns instead of generalizing**.
Lack of Parallelism	Each decision branch is computed **sequentially**, slowing down learning.
Memory Constraints	Storing full decision trees consumes **large amounts of memory**.

Quantum Decision Trees **overcome these limitations by leveraging quantum computing for faster decision-making**.

---

3. How Quantum Decision Trees Work

Quantum Decision Trees **replace classical recursive partitioning with quantum superposition and entanglement**, allowing **exponential parallelism in feature selection and classification**.

Key Enhancements of Quantum Decision Trees

Feature	Classical Decision Trees	Quantum Decision Trees (QDTs)
Feature Selection	Evaluates features sequentially	**Evaluates all features simultaneously** using superposition
Computational Speed	O(N log N) time complexity	**Exponential speedup** with quantum parallelism
Memory Efficiency	Requires **storing large decision trees**	Uses **quantum states to encode all splits efficiently**
Scalability	Struggles with **high-dimensional datasets**	Easily scales to **big data problems**
Training Process	Requires **greedy heuristics** for split selection	Uses **quantum circuit optimizations** for optimal split selection

Quantum Decision Trees improve **classification accuracy, feature selection speed, and scalability** compared to classical decision trees.

---

4. The Workflow of a Quantum Decision Tree

Step 1: Quantum Feature Encoding

- Classical data is converted into **quantum states** using **quantum encoding techniques** (Amplitude Encoding, Basis Encoding, etc.).
- Each data point is **represented as a qubit**.

Step 2: Quantum Superposition for Feature Evaluation

- Classical trees evaluate features **one at a time**.
- QDTs apply **superposition**, evaluating **multiple features in parallel**.

Step 3: Quantum Entanglement for Feature Dependencies

- Quantum entanglement captures **correlations between features** more effectively than classical models.
- This improves classification accuracy by **considering relationships between attributes**.

Step 4: Quantum Measurement for Classification

- The **quantum state collapses** into a classification decision.
- The final **predicted class is measured and converted into classical data**.

---

5. Mathematical Representation of Quantum Decision Trees

In classical decision trees, the **decision function** is based on:

$$y=f(x)=\sum_{i=1}^{n} w_i x_i + b$$

where:

- x_i are feature values.
- w_i are learned weights.
- b is the bias term.

In **Quantum Decision Trees**, the equivalent decision function is modeled as a **quantum transformation**:

$$| \psi_{\text{output}} \rangle = U(\theta) | \psi_{\text{input}} \rangle$$

where:

- $| \psi_{\text{input}} \rangle$ represents the quantum-encoded feature state.
- $U(\theta)$ is the quantum circuit that applies feature transformations.
- $| \psi_{\text{output}} \rangle$ is the final quantum state before measurement.

Quantum Decision Trees use **quantum gates** to process decisions exponentially faster than classical models.

---

6. Example: Quantum Decision Tree for Fraud Detection

Classical Decision Tree for Fraud Classification

plaintext
CopyEdit

```
    Is the transaction amount > $10,000?
          /              \
      Yes                No
      /                    \
  Is location unusual?  Is IP blacklisted?
   /          \          /          \
Fraud      Not Fraud   Fraud      Not Fraud
```

Quantum Decision Tree for Fraud Classification

plaintext
CopyEdit

```
Quantum Superposition Applied

            ↓
+---------------------------+
| Quantum Feature Mapping   |
+---------------------------+

            ↓
+----------------------------+
| Quantum Decision Tree Branch |
| (Simultaneous Feature Selection) |
+----------------------------+

            ↓
+------------------------+
| Quantum Measurement    |
+------------------------+
```

```
              ┆
+----------------------+
| Classification Output |
+----------------------+
```

In **Quantum Decision Trees**, all **decision splits happen simultaneously**, making fraud detection faster and more efficient.

7. Flowchart: Workflow of Quantum Supervised Learning

Below is the **step-by-step workflow of Quantum Supervised Learning** models, including Quantum Decision Trees and Quantum Support Vector Machines (QSVMs).

plaintext
CopyEdit
```
Start
  |
  |---> Classical Data Input
  |        (e.g., Images, Text, Financial Data)
  |
  |---> Quantum Feature Mapping
  |        (Basis Encoding, Amplitude Encoding, Angle Encoding)
  |
  |---> Train Quantum Supervised Learning Model
  |        (Quantum Decision Tree, QSVM, Quantum Neural Network)
  |
  |---> Quantum Computation
  |        (Superposition, Entanglement, Quantum Parallelism)
  |
  |---> Quantum Measurement
  |        (Extract Classical Predictions from Qubits)
  |
  |---> AI Model Prediction
  |        (Spam Detection, Image Classification, Fraud
Detection)
```

Key Highlights of the Flowchart

Quantum Feature Mapping replaces traditional feature selection.
Quantum Computation accelerates training using parallelism.
Quantum Measurement extracts final AI predictions efficiently.

8. Real-World Applications of Quantum Decision Trees

Application	How QDTs Improve Performance
Medical Diagnosis	Classifies diseases with **higher accuracy and efficiency**.
Fraud Detection	Detects fraudulent transactions **in real time**.
Quantum NLP (Natural Language Processing)	Enhances **text classification and sentiment analysis**.
Cybersecurity	Improves **threat detection and anomaly recognition**.

Quantum Decision Trees **outperform classical models** in **complex classification tasks** where **speed and accuracy are crucial**.

Quantum Decision Trees (QDTs) **redefine supervised learning models** by enabling:

Simultaneous feature selection using quantum superposition.
Faster and more scalable decision-making.
Higher classification accuracy for real-world AI applications.

As **quantum hardware improves**, Quantum Decision Trees will become **a vital component of AI-driven decision-making**, unlocking **new possibilities in deep learning, fraud detection, and medical diagnosis**.

Chapter 8

Quantum Unsupervised Learning Models

Unsupervised learning is a key branch of machine learning where the model identifies patterns, structures, and relationships in data without explicit labels. In classical machine learning, algorithms such as **K-Means Clustering, Principal Component Analysis (PCA), and Hierarchical Clustering** are widely used for exploratory data analysis and dimensionality reduction.

Quantum computing enhances unsupervised learning by leveraging **quantum superposition, entanglement, and parallelism** to process high-dimensional data more efficiently. Quantum Unsupervised Learning models are being explored for **big data analytics, feature extraction, and data clustering** in various domains, including finance, healthcare, and cybersecurity.

This chapter delves into **Quantum K-Means Clustering, Quantum Principal Component Analysis (QPCA), and their advantages over classical approaches**.

Introduction to Unsupervised Learning in Quantum AI

1. The Role of Unsupervised Learning in AI

Unlike supervised learning, which relies on labeled datasets, **unsupervised learning models** detect hidden patterns and structures in raw data. These models are extensively used in:

- **Clustering:** Grouping similar data points (e.g., customer segmentation in marketing).
- **Dimensionality Reduction:** Reducing the number of features while retaining key information (e.g., image compression).
- **Anomaly Detection:** Identifying rare events or fraud in large datasets (e.g., financial fraud detection).

Unsupervised learning **faces computational challenges** when processing large datasets, as clustering and dimensionality reduction methods require extensive matrix operations and distance calculations. Quantum AI **enhances these tasks by processing multiple possibilities simultaneously**.

2. How Quantum Computing Enhances Unsupervised Learning

Quantum Parallelism for Faster Computation

Quantum computers process **exponentially large feature spaces** in parallel, accelerating unsupervised learning tasks like clustering and PCA.

Quantum Superposition for Feature Representation

Instead of encoding data as binary numbers, quantum states allow for richer feature mappings, improving clustering efficiency.

Quantum Entanglement for Improved Correlations

Quantum entanglement enables **better feature extraction**, allowing the algorithm to detect hidden patterns **more efficiently** than classical methods.

Quantum Speedup for Large-Scale Data Analysis

Quantum AI models can **solve optimization problems in fewer steps**, leading to significant speed improvements in clustering and principal component analysis.

Quantum K-Means Clustering for Big Data

1. Overview of Classical K-Means Clustering

101

K-Means clustering is one of the most widely used unsupervised learning algorithms. It partitions data into **K clusters** by iteratively updating cluster centroids. The algorithm follows these steps:

1. **Initialize K centroids** randomly.
2. **Assign each data point** to the nearest centroid.
3. **Recalculate centroids** based on new cluster assignments.
4. **Repeat steps 2-3 until convergence** (centroids no longer change).

However, K-Means **faces scalability issues** when handling large datasets due to the computational complexity of **distance calculations** and iterative updates.

---

2. Quantum K-Means: How It Works

Quantum K-Means clustering leverages **quantum distance computation and quantum state representation** to improve efficiency. The key steps include:

Step 1: Quantum State Encoding of Data Points

- Classical data points are encoded into **quantum states** using **Quantum Feature Mapping**.
- Each data point $|x\rangle$ is mapped into a **high-dimensional Hilbert space**, enabling faster similarity calculations.

Step 2: Quantum Superposition for Distance Calculation

- Classical K-Means requires computing the Euclidean distance for each data point against every centroid.
- Quantum K-Means **leverages superposition** to compute **all distances simultaneously**, reducing complexity from **O(NK)** to **O(log N)**.

Step 3: Quantum Measurement for Cluster Assignment

- The algorithm assigns each data point to the closest quantum centroid based on **quantum probability distributions**.

Step 4: Iterative Update of Quantum Centroids

- Centroids are updated iteratively using **quantum variational circuits**, improving clustering efficiency.

3. Advantages of Quantum K-Means Over Classical K-Means

Feature	Classical K-Means	Quantum K-Means
Computational Complexity	$O(NK)$	$O(\log N)$
Distance Calculation	Iterative, costly	Parallelized via quantum states
Scalability	Limited for large datasets	Handles high-dimensional data efficiently
Feature Mapping	Limited to Euclidean space	Quantum-enhanced feature mapping
Convergence Speed	Slower for large datasets	Faster convergence with quantum circuits

Quantum K-Means is particularly useful in **big data clustering, customer segmentation, and anomaly detection**, offering **exponential speedup** in large-scale machine learning problems.

Quantum Principal Component Analysis (QPCA)

1. Overview of Classical PCA

Principal Component Analysis (PCA) is a fundamental dimensionality reduction technique used in AI. It transforms high-dimensional data into a **lower-dimensional space** while preserving essential information.

How Classical PCA Works:

1. **Compute the Covariance Matrix:** Measures how features vary together.
2. **Eigenvalue Decomposition:** Extracts principal components from eigenvectors.
3. **Transform Data:** Projects data onto principal components to reduce dimensionality.

PCA is widely used in **image compression, gene expression analysis, and feature extraction**. However, its **computational cost increases with large datasets**, especially when performing **eigenvalue decomposition on high-dimensional matrices**.

---

2. Quantum PCA: How It Works

Quantum Principal Component Analysis (QPCA) **enhances PCA by leveraging quantum parallelism** to perform eigenvalue decomposition efficiently.

Step 1: Quantum Encoding of Data Covariance Matrix

- Classical data is encoded into a **quantum density matrix**.
- Quantum PCA estimates the **eigenvalues and eigenvectors** of the covariance matrix.

Step 2: Quantum Eigenvalue Estimation

- Classical PCA requires solving **large matrix eigenvalue problems**, which is computationally expensive.
- Quantum PCA uses **Quantum Phase Estimation (QPE)** to estimate eigenvalues exponentially faster.

Step 3: Projection onto Principal Components

- Data is projected onto **quantum principal components**, reducing dimensionality while **retaining essential information**.

---

3. Advantages of Quantum PCA Over Classical PCA

Feature	Classical PCA	Quantum PCA
Eigenvalue Computation	Requires matrix diagonalization	Uses quantum phase estimation
Computational Complexity	$O(N^3)$ for large datasets	$O(\log N)$ using quantum speedup
Scalability	Limited for high-dimensional data	Efficient for large feature spaces
Feature Transformation	Linear projections	Quantum-enhanced transformations
Energy Efficiency	High computational cost	Lower resource consumption

Quantum PCA is valuable in **image processing, genomic analysis, and financial modeling**, where dimensionality reduction is essential for improving AI model efficiency.

Illustration: Quantum Clustering vs. Classical Clustering

A comparative visualization of Quantum K-Means and Classical K-Means demonstrates how quantum algorithms efficiently cluster data using fewer computational steps.

1. **Classical K-Means requires multiple iterations to converge** due to sequential distance calculations.
2. **Quantum K-Means processes all distance calculations simultaneously**, leading to faster convergence.
3. **Quantum PCA enables real-time dimensionality reduction**, improving machine learning performance in high-dimensional spaces.

By leveraging **quantum superposition, entanglement, and parallelism**, Quantum AI models redefine the capabilities of **unsupervised learning**.

The next section will explore **Quantum Reinforcement Learning (QRL) and how quantum-enhanced agents learn in dynamic environments**.

Chapter 9

Quantum Reinforcement Learning (QRL)

Quantum Reinforcement Learning (QRL) is a **cutting-edge field** that combines **quantum computing** and **reinforcement learning (RL)** to create **intelligent quantum agents** capable of learning from their environment. Unlike traditional machine learning, which primarily relies on supervised and unsupervised techniques, **reinforcement learning enables AI agents to make sequential decisions, explore environments, and optimize rewards over time**.

QRL **leverages quantum mechanics** to enhance RL algorithms, enabling **faster learning, better optimization, and improved decision-making in complex environments**.

The Basics of Reinforcement Learning

1. What is Reinforcement Learning?

Reinforcement Learning (RL) is a **learning paradigm** in artificial intelligence where an agent interacts with an environment and learns to **maximize cumulative rewards over time**. Unlike supervised learning, which requires labeled datasets, RL agents **explore, experiment, and adapt** through trial and error.

Key Components of RL

1. **Agent** → The learning entity (e.g., a robot, an AI model, or a trading bot).
2. **Environment** → The external system with which the agent interacts.
3. **State (sss)** → A representation of the environment at a given moment.
4. **Action (aaa)** → A choice made by the agent to influence the environment.
5. **Reward (RRR)** → A feedback signal indicating how good an action was.

6. **Policy (π\piπ)** → A strategy that defines how the agent selects actions.
7. **Value Function (V(s)V(s)V(s))** → A function estimating the expected long-term rewards for a given state.

---

2. How RL Works: The Markov Decision Process (MDP)

Reinforcement Learning is typically modeled using a **Markov Decision Process (MDP)**, defined as:

$(S,A,P,R,γ)(S, A, P, R, \gamma)(S,A,P,R,γ)$

where:

- **SSS** → Set of possible states.
- **AAA** → Set of possible actions.
- **P(s'|s,a)P(s' | s, a)P(s'|s,a)** → Probability of transitioning from state sss to s's's' after action aaa.
- **R(s,a)R(s, a)R(s,a)** → Immediate reward function.
- **γ\gammaγ** → Discount factor (balances immediate vs. future rewards).

The RL Workflow

plaintext
CopyEdit
```
1. The agent observes the environment state (s)
2. The agent selects an action (a) based on its policy (π)
3. The environment responds with:
   - A new state (s')
   - A reward (R)
4. The agent updates its policy to maximize cumulative rewards
5. Repeat until convergence
```

---

3. Challenges in Classical Reinforcement Learning

Despite its effectiveness, classical RL faces **significant computational challenges**:

Challenge	Impact
Curse of Dimensionality	RL models struggle with **large state-action spaces**.
Slow Convergence	Training deep RL models requires **millions of episodes**.
Computational Cost	RL algorithms rely on **powerful GPUs and parallelization**.
Exploration vs. Exploitation Trade-off	Balancing **new knowledge exploration** vs. **exploiting learned knowledge** is complex.

Quantum Reinforcement Learning (QRL) **addresses these challenges by utilizing quantum parallelism and superposition**, allowing **exponentially faster decision-making**.

How Quantum Agents Learn in QRL

Quantum Reinforcement Learning (QRL) introduces **quantum agents**—learning systems that leverage **quantum-enhanced state representations, faster policy optimization, and improved decision-making**.

Unlike classical agents, **quantum agents use qubits instead of classical bits** for storing and processing information, leading to **exponential speedup and improved efficiency**.

---

1. The Role of Quantum Mechanics in QRL

Quantum computing enhances RL by introducing **three fundamental quantum properties**:

109

Quantum Principle	Impact on RL
Superposition	Enables agents to explore **multiple states simultaneously**, accelerating training.
Entanglement	Allows for **better correlation between state-action pairs**, improving policy learning.
Quantum Tunneling	Helps **avoid local optima** in reinforcement learning tasks.

These principles **boost exploration capabilities** and allow **more efficient optimization of policies**.

---

2. Quantum State Representation in QRL

In classical RL, the agent represents states as **high-dimensional feature vectors**. However, QRL **encodes states into quantum wave functions**, reducing memory overhead and allowing more complex state representations.

Quantum State Encoding

A classical state vector:

$$|s\rangle = [s_1, s_2, ..., s_n]$$

is transformed into a **quantum superposition state**:

$$|\psi_s\rangle = \sum_i \alpha_i | s_i \rangle$$

where α_i are probability amplitudes. This **enables parallel processing of multiple states**, improving learning efficiency.

3. Quantum Policy Optimization

Quantum Policy Representation

In classical RL, a policy is a function:

$$\pi(s)=a\pi(s) = a\pi(s)=a$$

mapping states sss to actions aaa.

In QRL, a **quantum policy function** is represented as a **unitary transformation**:

$$U\pi\,|\,s\rangle=|a\rangle U\_\pi\,|\,s \rangle = |\,a\,\rangle U\pi\,|\,s\rangle=|a\rangle$$

This means the quantum agent **learns an optimal policy using quantum circuit transformations**, which improves **decision-making speed and efficiency**.

Quantum Policy Gradient

The policy gradient optimization process in QRL follows:

$$\theta t+1=\theta t-\eta\partial L\partial\theta t\theta\_{t+1} = \theta\_t - \eta \frac{\partial L}{\partial \theta\_t}\theta t+1=\theta t-\eta\partial\theta t\partial L$$

where $\theta\theta\theta$ represents the trainable parameters of a **quantum variational circuit**.

This approach ensures **faster convergence and better optimization** of RL models.

---

4. Quantum Exploration Strategies in RL

One of the biggest challenges in RL is balancing **exploration (trying new actions) and exploitation (using learned strategies)**. Quantum Reinforcement Learning introduces **quantum-enhanced exploration techniques**:

Quantum Grover's Search for Efficient Exploration

Grover's search algorithm provides **quadratic speedup** in exploring **large action spaces**, improving an agent's ability to discover optimal actions faster.

Quantum Annealing for Policy Optimization

Quantum annealing helps **avoid local optima** by allowing **quantum tunneling through bad solutions**, leading to **more optimal policies**.

---

5. Quantum Q-Learning Algorithm

Classical Q-learning updates a Q-table using:

$$Q(s,a)=Q(s,a)+\alpha[R+\gamma maxaQ(s',a)-Q(s,a)]Q(s, a) = Q(s, a) + \alpha [R + \gamma \max_a Q(s', a) - Q(s, a)]Q(s,a)=Q(s,a)+\alpha[R+\gamma amaxQ(s',a)-Q(s,a)]$$

In QRL, the **quantum-enhanced Q-function** is updated using **quantum states**:

$$|Q(s,a)\rangle = UQ(s,a)| Q(s, a) \rangle = U Q(s, a)|Q(s,a)\rangle=UQ(s,a)$$

where **UUU** represents quantum state transformations, enabling **exponential speedup in updating value functions**.

---

6. Applications of Quantum Reinforcement Learning

Application	How QRL Improves Performance
Autonomous Vehicles	Enhances real-time decision-making in self-driving cars.
Quantum Robotics	Optimizes robot learning tasks **with faster state-action processing**.
Financial Trading AI	Improves stock market predictions using **quantum portfolio optimization**.
Healthcare & Drug Discovery	Helps AI agents **find optimal treatment plans** more efficiently.

Quantum RL provides **unprecedented advantages in AI-driven decision-making**, making it a **powerful tool for future intelligent systems**.

Quantum Reinforcement Learning (QRL) is **revolutionizing AI decision-making** by leveraging quantum mechanics for **faster learning, better exploration, and optimized policies**.

 Quantum Agents use superposition and entanglement to learn efficiently.
  Quantum Policy Optimization allows exponential speedup in decision-making.
  Quantum Q-Learning enables faster convergence for reinforcement learning models.

As quantum computing continues to advance, **Quantum RL will become the foundation for AI-driven autonomous systems, robotics, and complex decision-making tasks**.

Quantum Markov Decision Processes (QMDPs)

1. Introduction to Quantum Markov Decision Processes

Quantum Markov Decision Processes (QMDPs) are the **quantum-enhanced version** of classical **Markov Decision Processes (MDPs)** used in **reinforcement learning (RL)**. They provide a **framework for quantum agents** to learn and make sequential decisions **more efficiently than classical RL models**.

Traditional **MDPs suffer from computational bottlenecks** when handling **large state-action spaces**, requiring **significant memory and processing power**. Quantum MDPs **overcome these challenges** by leveraging **quantum superposition, entanglement, and quantum state transitions**, enabling **exponentially faster decision-making**.

2. How Classical Markov Decision Processes Work

An MDP is a **mathematical framework** used in RL for **decision-making** under uncertainty. It consists of:

$(S,A,P,R,\gamma)(S, A, P, R, \gamma)(S,A,P,R,\gamma)$

where:

- **SSS** → Set of possible states.
- **AAA** → Set of possible actions.
- **P(s'|s,a)P(s' | s, a)P(s'|s,a)** → Transition probability of moving from state sss to s's's' after taking action aaa.
- **R(s,a)R(s, a)R(s,a)** → Reward function for taking action aaa in state sss.
- **γ\gammaγ** → Discount factor for balancing immediate vs. future rewards.

Classical MDP Workflow

plaintext
CopyEdit

```
1. Agent observes the current state (s).
2. The agent selects an action (a) based on its policy (π).
3. The environment transitions to a new state (s') based on
probability P(s' | s, a).
4. The agent receives a reward R(s, a).
5. The process repeats until the agent learns an optimal
policy.
```

MDPs **optimize sequential decision-making** but become computationally expensive as **state-action spaces grow**.

---

3. Quantum Markov Decision Processes (QMDPs)

QMDPs extend classical MDPs by encoding **states, actions, and transition probabilities** into **quantum states**, leveraging **quantum parallelism and entanglement** for enhanced decision-making.

How QMDPs Improve Classical MDPs

Feature	Classical MDP	Quantum MDP (QMDP)
State Representation	Classical probability distributions	Quantum superposition of multiple states
Computational Complexity	**O(N)** for state transitions	**Exponential speedup** with quantum parallelism
Policy Optimization	Requires extensive iterations	Uses **quantum Grover search** for faster policy learning
Memory Efficiency	Stores large transition matrices	Uses **quantum state encoding**, reducing memory needs

QMDPs enable **faster decision-making** by encoding **state transitions and actions into quantum wave functions, allowing parallel evaluation** of multiple possibilities.

---

4. Quantum State Representation in QMDPs

In QMDPs, **states are stored as quantum superposition states** instead of discrete probability distributions:

$$|S\rangle = \sum_i \alpha_i | s_i \rangle$$

where:

- $|S\rangle$ represents a **superposition of multiple states**.
- α_i are probability amplitudes.

Quantum Transition Probabilities

Instead of using classical probability matrices, QMDPs use **quantum unitary transformations** to model state transitions:

$$|S'\rangle = U | S \rangle$$

where:

- U is a **quantum operator** encoding **state transitions**.

This approach **reduces computational complexity** by **processing multiple state transitions simultaneously**.

5. Quantum Policy Optimization in QMDPs

In classical RL, an optimal policy is found by maximizing:

$$V^\pi (s) = \mathbb{E} \left[\sum_{t=0}^{\infty} \gamma^t R_t \right]$$

In QMDPs, **quantum reinforcement learning optimizes policies using variational quantum circuits (VQCs)**:

$$|\pi\rangle = U_\pi | S \rangle$$

where:

- U_π is a **trainable quantum circuit** encoding the optimal policy.
- The agent **adjusts U_π iteratively using quantum gradient descent**.

This approach **accelerates reinforcement learning** by **allowing quantum agents to explore multiple policies simultaneously**.

---

6. Quantum Q-Learning Algorithm for QMDPs

Classical Q-learning updates the Q-value function as:

$$Q(s, a) = Q(s, a) + \alpha [R + \gamma \max_{a'} Q(s', a') - Q(s, a)]$$

Quantum Q-learning replaces this with **quantum-enhanced state transitions**:

116

$$|Q(s,a)\rangle = UQ(s,a)| \ Q(s, a) \text{ \textbackslash rangle} = U \ Q(s, a)|Q(s,a)\rangle = UQ(s,a)$$

where:

- **UUU** is a quantum transformation encoding state-action values.
- The Q-function is stored in a **quantum register** instead of a classical table.

This provides **exponential speedup in computing Q-values**, leading to **faster learning rates in complex environments**.

Case Study: Quantum Reinforcement Learning in Financial Optimization

1. Problem Statement

Financial markets require **real-time decision-making** to optimize trading strategies. Traditional **reinforcement learning models** struggle with:

- **High-dimensional data** (thousands of stocks, options, and commodities).
- **Non-linear price movements** (complex relationships between market variables).
- **Computational inefficiency** (high training costs for deep RL models).

Quantum RL (QRL) can **enhance financial decision-making** by:
 Speeding up learning of optimal trading policies.
 Handling large-scale portfolio optimization tasks.
 Improving risk assessment using quantum uncertainty modeling.

---

2. Quantum RL Approach to Financial Markets

A **quantum trading agent** can be modeled using a **Quantum Markov Decision Process (QMDP)**:

$$(S,A,P,R,\gamma)(S, A, P, R, \text{ \textbackslash gamma})(S,A,P,R,\gamma)$$

where:

117

- **SSS** → Market states (e.g., stock prices, volatility, interest rates).
- **AAA** → Actions (buy, sell, hold).
- **P(s'|s,a)P(s' | s, a)P(s'|s,a)** → Quantum-enhanced transition probabilities.
- **R(s,a)R(s, a)R(s,a)** → Reward function based on market gains/losses.
- **γ\gammaγ** → Discount factor balancing short-term vs. long-term rewards.

Workflow of Quantum RL for Trading

plaintext
CopyEdit

```
1. The quantum agent observes the current market state (stock
prices, indicators).
2. Quantum superposition enables simultaneous exploration of
multiple trading actions.
3. The quantum circuit selects the optimal action (buy, sell,
hold) using Grover's search.
4. The financial environment responds with a new state (price
fluctuations).
5. The quantum agent updates its strategy using Q-learning.
6. The process repeats to refine the optimal trading policy.
```

3. Advantages of Quantum RL in Financial Optimization

Feature	Classical RL in Finance	Quantum RL in Finance
Computational Speed	Slow training on large datasets	**Faster policy optimization** using quantum search
Market Complexity	Requires deep learning models	Uses **quantum-enhanced state encoding**
Portfolio Optimization	Limited by classical search algorithms	Uses **quantum Grover's search for faster risk assessment**

Adaptability to Market Shifts	Slow response to market volatility	Quantum parallelism allows real-time adjustments

By **applying Quantum RL to financial trading**, hedge funds, banks, and investors **can optimize trading strategies with unprecedented efficiency.**

Quantum Markov Decision Processes (QMDPs) and Quantum RL **redefine how AI agents learn and make sequential decisions.**

 QMDPs leverage quantum superposition for faster decision-making.
 Quantum Policy Optimization accelerates learning in RL models.
 Quantum RL improves financial trading strategies, risk assessment, and portfolio optimization.

As quantum computing matures, **Quantum RL will revolutionize AI-driven decision-making in finance, healthcare, robotics, and autonomous systems.**

The next section will explore **Quantum Deep Reinforcement Learning (QDRL) and Real-World QRL Applications.**

Chapter 10

Getting Started with Quantum Machine Learning

Quantum Machine Learning (QML) is an **emerging field that integrates quantum computing with artificial intelligence** to solve complex problems more efficiently. While traditional machine learning relies on **classical hardware**, QML utilizes **quantum algorithms and quantum circuits** to enhance data processing and pattern recognition.

Before developing quantum machine learning models, you need to **set up a proper quantum computing development environment**. This chapter provides a **step-by-step guide** on setting up **Qiskit, Cirq, and PennyLane**, the three most widely used quantum programming frameworks.

Setting Up a QML Development Environment

1. Choosing a Quantum Programming Framework

Quantum computing development requires **specialized software libraries** that allow interaction with quantum processors. The three most popular frameworks are:

Framework	Developer	Best Use Case
Qiskit	IBM	Universal quantum computing & QML development
Cirq	Google	Quantum circuit simulation & hardware control
PennyLane	Xanadu	Hybrid quantum-classical machine learning

Each framework has unique strengths, and depending on the use case, you may choose **one or multiple frameworks**.

2. Setting Up a Quantum Computing Environment

To begin with **Quantum Machine Learning (QML) development**, you need:

1. **Python 3.x installed** (most quantum frameworks are built for Python).
2. **A quantum computing SDK** (Qiskit, Cirq, or PennyLane).
3. **A simulator or access to real quantum hardware** (IBM Quantum, Google Quantum AI, or Xanadu's cloud platform).
4. **An IDE (Jupyter Notebook, VS Code, or PyCharm) for writing quantum programs**.

Installing and Configuring Qiskit, Cirq, and PennyLane

1. Installing Qiskit

Qiskit is **IBM's open-source quantum computing framework** that allows developers to **build, simulate, and execute quantum circuits** on IBM's quantum processors.

Step 1: Install Qiskit

Open a terminal or command prompt and install Qiskit using pip:

bash
CopyEdit
```
pip install qiskit
```

To install Qiskit with visualization and machine learning support, use:

bash

```
pip install qiskit[visualization] qiskit-machine-learning
```

Step 2: Verify Installation

After installation, check if Qiskit is installed correctly:

python

```
import qiskit
print(qiskit.__version__)
```

If the version prints successfully, Qiskit is installed.

Step 3: Install IBM Quantum Provider

To run quantum programs on IBM's **real quantum computers**, install the IBM Quantum Provider:

bash

```
pip install qiskit-ibm-runtime
```

Then, import and set up your IBM Quantum account:

python

```
from qiskit_ibm_runtime import QiskitRuntimeService
QiskitRuntimeService.save_account("YOUR_IBM_QUANTUM_API_KEY")
```

Step 4: Running a Simple Quantum Circuit in Qiskit

python

```
from qiskit import QuantumCircuit, Aer, transpile, assemble,
execute

# Create a simple quantum circuit with 1 qubit
qc = QuantumCircuit(1)
qc.h(0)  # Apply Hadamard gate

# Simulate the circuit
simulator = Aer.get_backend('statevector_simulator')
result = execute(qc, simulator).result()

# Print the quantum state
print(result.get_statevector())
```

If you see a quantum state output, Qiskit is configured successfully.

---

2. Installing Cirq

Cirq is **Google's quantum computing framework** designed for **building and simulating quantum circuits** on Google's Sycamore quantum processor.

Step 1: Install Cirq
bash
CopyEdit
```
pip install cirq
```

Step 2: Verify Installation
python
CopyEdit
```
import cirq
print(cirq.__version__)
```

If the version prints successfully, Cirq is installed.

Step 3: Running a Simple Quantum Circuit in Cirq

python
CopyEdit

```python
import cirq

# Define a qubit
qubit = cirq.GridQubit(0, 0)

# Create a quantum circuit
circuit = cirq.Circuit()
circuit.append(cirq.H(qubit))  # Apply Hadamard gate
circuit.append(cirq.measure(qubit))  # Measure the qubit

# Simulate the circuit
simulator = cirq.Simulator()
result = simulator.run(circuit, repetitions=10)

# Print measurement results
print(result)
```

If you see a measurement output, Cirq is configured correctly.

3. Installing PennyLane

PennyLane is **Xanadu's quantum machine learning framework**, designed for **hybrid quantum-classical machine learning** using variational quantum circuits.

Step 1: Install PennyLane

bash
CopyEdit

```bash
pip install pennylane
```

For full machine learning support, install:
124

```bash
bash
CopyEdit
pip install pennylane[pytorch] pennylane[tensorflow]
```

Step 2: Verify Installation

```python
python
CopyEdit
import pennylane as qml
print(qml.__version__)
```

Step 3: Running a Simple Quantum Machine Learning Model in PennyLane

```python
python
CopyEdit
import pennylane as qml
import numpy as np

# Define a quantum device (simulator)
dev = qml.device("default.qubit", wires=1)

# Define a quantum circuit (QNode)
@qml.qnode(dev)
def quantum_circuit(theta):
    qml.RX(theta, wires=0)
    return qml.expval(qml.PauliZ(0))

# Run the circuit with a parameter
theta = np.pi / 4
result = quantum_circuit(theta)

print(f"Quantum Expectation Value: {result}")
```

If you see a quantum expectation value, PennyLane is set up successfully.

125

Comparison of Qiskit, Cirq, and PennyLane

Feature	Qiskit (IBM)	Cirq (Google)	PennyLane (Xanadu)
Quantum Circuit Simulation	Yes	Yes	Yes
Real Quantum Hardware Access	IBM Quantum	Google Quantum AI	Xanadu's Quantum Cloud
Machine Learning Support	Qiskit ML	Limited	Deep Learning (TensorFlow, PyTorch)
Ease of Use			
Best Use Case	Universal quantum computing	Hardware-specific optimization	Hybrid quantum-classical ML

Each framework has **strengths and limitations**, and many developers **use multiple frameworks** depending on their use cases.

4. Best Practices for Quantum Machine Learning Development

- **Use Jupyter Notebooks** for interactive QML development.
- **Test on Quantum Simulators First** before running on real quantum hardware.

- **Optimize Circuits** to reduce quantum gate errors and noise.
- **Utilize Hybrid Quantum-Classical Models** using PennyLane for deep learning integration.
- **Stay Updated** with the latest quantum research and hardware improvements.

Setting up a **Quantum Machine Learning (QML) development environment** is the first step towards building **quantum-enhanced AI models**. With **Qiskit, Cirq, and PennyLane**, developers can:

Design and simulate quantum circuits efficiently.
Train quantum machine learning models using hybrid frameworks.
Run experiments on real quantum processors.

As quantum computing evolves, these tools will enable **next-generation AI breakthroughs**, revolutionizing fields like **finance, healthcare, and cryptography**.

The next section will explore **Building Your First Quantum Machine Learning Model** using Qiskit, Cirq, and PennyLane.

Running Your First Quantum AI Model

Now that we have set up the **Quantum Machine Learning (QML) development environment** with **Qiskit, Cirq, and PennyLane**, the next step is to **build and run a Quantum AI model**. This section will guide you through:

Implementing a simple Quantum Neural Network (QNN)
Training a Quantum Machine Learning model
Executing the model on a quantum simulator

This will provide **hands-on experience** with **Quantum AI** and demonstrate the power of **hybrid quantum-classical learning**.

1. Overview of Quantum AI Models

127

Quantum AI models are different from classical AI models because they use **quantum states and quantum circuits** instead of traditional **neurons and weights**. The most commonly used **Quantum AI architectures** include:

Quantum AI Model	Description	Use Cases
Quantum Neural Networks (QNNs)	Quantum circuits act as neural network layers	Image classification, AI optimization
Quantum Support Vector Machines (QSVMs)	Quantum kernels enhance classical SVMs	Fraud detection, NLP, finance
Quantum Variational Circuits	Parameterized quantum circuits optimize AI models	Quantum-enhanc ed deep learning
Quantum Generative Models	Quantum-enhanced GANs and Boltzmann machines	AI-generated data, security models

Each of these models uses **quantum superposition, entanglement, and parallelism** to achieve **exponential speedup and improved efficiency**.

2. Running Your First Quantum Neural Network (QNN) in Qiskit

A **Quantum Neural Network (QNN)** is a **variational quantum circuit (VQC)** that mimics classical neural networks. It consists of **trainable quantum gates**, where the parameters are optimized during training.

Step 1: Import Required Libraries

python
CopyEdit

```
import numpy as np
from qiskit import QuantumCircuit, Aer, transpile, assemble, execute
from qiskit.circuit import Parameter
```

```
from qiskit_machine_learning.neural_networks import CircuitQNN
from qiskit_machine_learning.connectors import TorchConnector
import torch
import torch.nn as nn
```

Step 2: Define a Quantum Circuit for the QNN

python
CopyEdit
```
# Define quantum circuit with trainable parameter
theta = Parameter('θ')
qc = QuantumCircuit(1)
qc.rx(theta, 0)  # Rotation gate as trainable parameter

# Visualize the circuit
qc.draw()
```

This **Quantum Neural Network** contains:

- **One qubit**
- **A trainable RX gate (parameter θ)**
- **Quantum circuit representation of a single-layer QNN**

Step 3: Convert the Circuit into a Quantum Neural Network

python
CopyEdit
```
# Define Quantum Neural Network (QNN)
quantum_neural_net = CircuitQNN(qc, input_params=[],
weight_params=[theta], interpret=lambda x: x)

# Convert Quantum Model to PyTorch Compatible Network
qnn_model = TorchConnector(quantum_neural_net)
```

This step **transforms the quantum circuit into a neural network layer**, allowing integration with **PyTorch-based AI models**.

Step 4: Define a Hybrid Quantum-Classical AI Model

python
CopyEdit

```python
# Define a simple quantum-classical hybrid model
class HybridQNN(nn.Module):
    def __init__(self):
        super().__init__()
        self.fc1 = nn.Linear(1, 4)  # Classical layer
        self.qnn = qnn_model  # Quantum Neural Network Layer
        self.fc2 = nn.Linear(2, 1)  # Classical output layer

    def forward(self, x):
        x = torch.relu(self.fc1(x))
        x = self.qnn(x)
        x = torch.sigmoid(self.fc2(x))
        return x

# Initialize the model
model = HybridQNN()
```

Here, we integrate:

- **A classical input layer**
- **A quantum neural network layer**
- **A classical output layer**

This **hybrid approach** takes advantage of both **classical deep learning** and **quantum processing**.

Step 5: Train the Quantum Neural Network

python
CopyEdit

```python
# Define optimizer and loss function
optimizer = torch.optim.Adam(model.parameters(), lr=0.01)
loss_function = nn.MSELoss()

# Generate sample training data
X_train = torch.tensor([[0.1], [0.5], [0.9]],
dtype=torch.float32)
Y_train = torch.tensor([[0.2], [0.7], [1.0]],
dtype=torch.float32)

# Training loop
epochs = 100
for epoch in range(epochs):
    optimizer.zero_grad()
    output = model(X_train)
    loss = loss_function(output, Y_train)
    loss.backward()
    optimizer.step()

    if epoch % 10 == 0:
        print(f"Epoch {epoch}: Loss = {loss.item()}")

print("Training complete!")
```

This **trains the Quantum Neural Network** using PyTorch while **optimizing the quantum circuit parameters**.

Step 6: Run the Quantum Model on a Quantum Simulator

python
CopyEdit
```python
# Simulate the QNN on Aer backend
backend = Aer.get_backend('qasm_simulator')

# Execute the circuit
qobj = assemble(transpile(qc, backend))
result = backend.run(qobj).result()
```

```
# Display results
print(result.get_counts())
```

This runs the **Quantum AI model** on a **simulated quantum processor**, ensuring that everything is functioning properly.

---

3. Overview of QML Python Libraries

Several **Python libraries** support **Quantum Machine Learning (QML)**. Here's an overview:

Library	Developer	Primary Use	Quantum Hardware Support
Qiskit	IBM	Universal quantum computing & ML	IBM Quantum Cloud
Cirq	Google	Quantum circuit simulation & ML	Google Sycamore
PennyLane	Xanadu	Hybrid quantum-classical deep learning	Xanadu Cloud
TensorFlow Quantum (TFQ)	Google	Quantum ML with TensorFlow	Google Quantum AI
QuTiP	Open-source	Quantum computing research & ML	Simulations only

Each library specializes in **different aspects of quantum computing**. Developers often **combine multiple frameworks** to leverage the **best features**.

4. Running Your First Quantum AI Model in PennyLane

PennyLane allows for **hybrid quantum-classical deep learning**. Let's run a **simple Quantum Perceptron**:

```python
CopyEdit
import pennylane as qml
import numpy as np

# Define a quantum device with 2 qubits
dev = qml.device("default.qubit", wires=2)

# Define a quantum perceptron model
@qml.qnode(dev)
def quantum_perceptron(inputs, weights):
    qml.RX(inputs[0], wires=0)
    qml.RY(inputs[1], wires=1)
    qml.CNOT(wires=[0, 1])
    qml.RX(weights[0], wires=0)
    qml.RY(weights[1], wires=1)
    return qml.expval(qml.PauliZ(1))

# Initialize inputs and weights
inputs = np.array([0.1, 0.5])
weights = np.array([0.2, 0.8])

# Run the quantum perceptron
output = quantum_perceptron(inputs, weights)
print(f"Quantum Perceptron Output: {output}")
```

This model **demonstrates how quantum circuits** can be used for **machine learning tasks**.

Running **Quantum AI models** requires **combining classical deep learning techniques with quantum computing principles**. By implementing **Quantum Neural Networks (QNNs) and Quantum Perceptrons**, we can:

Train AI models faster using quantum circuits.
Leverage quantum parallelism for enhanced efficiency.
Integrate classical deep learning with quantum computing for hybrid AI solutions.

As quantum hardware continues to advance, **Quantum AI will play a major role in the future of deep learning and artificial intelligence**.

The next section will explore **Building Advanced QML Applications** and applying Quantum AI in **real-world scenarios like healthcare, finance, and cybersecurity**.

Chapter 11

Building a Quantum Classifier

Quantum classification models are a crucial application of **Quantum Machine Learning (QML)**. By leveraging the principles of **quantum computing**, quantum classifiers can **process high-dimensional data more efficiently** than classical machine learning models.

In this chapter, we will explore:

 Step-by-step guide to implementing a Quantum Support Vector Machine (QSVM)
  Hybrid Quantum-Classical AI models for improved efficiency
  Python implementation of a Quantum Classifier

These techniques enable **exponential speedup in classification tasks**, making them valuable for applications in **finance, medicine, cybersecurity, and beyond**.

Step-by-Step Guide to Implementing a Quantum SVM

1. What is a Quantum Support Vector Machine (QSVM)?

A **Support Vector Machine (SVM)** is a supervised learning algorithm that classifies data by finding the **optimal hyperplane** that separates different classes.
135

Classical SVM vs. Quantum SVM (QSVM)

Feature	Classical SVM	Quantum SVM (QSVM)
Feature Encoding	Uses numerical feature vectors	Encodes data into **quantum states**
Kernel Trick	Uses **RBF, polynomial, or linear kernels**	Uses **Quantum Kernel Methods**
Complexity	**Slow** for high-dimensional data	**Exponential speedup** using quantum parallelism
Scalability	Struggles with large datasets	Efficient for **big data and non-linear problems**

A **Quantum SVM (QSVM)** enhances classical SVMs by **mapping data into quantum feature spaces**, making classification **more accurate and efficient**.

---

2. How QSVM Works

Quantum SVMs operate using **Quantum Kernel Estimation**, which replaces classical kernel functions with **quantum-enhanced feature spaces**.

Mathematical Representation

A classical kernel function is:

$K(x_i, x_j) = \phi(x_i) \cdot \phi(x_j)$

where $\phi(x)$ represents the **feature transformation**.

In a **Quantum SVM (QSVM)**, the quantum kernel function is:

$K_Q(x_i, x_j) = |\langle \psi(x_i) | \psi(x_j) \rangle|^2$

where $|\psi(x)\rangle$ is the **quantum feature mapping** of xxx.

136

Quantum kernels enable the model to **classify data in exponentially large feature spaces without explicitly computing them.**

---

3. Steps to Build a Quantum SVM (QSVM)

Step 1: Encode Data into Quantum States

- Convert classical input features into **quantum feature maps** using **basis encoding, amplitude encoding, or angle encoding.**

Step 2: Construct a Quantum Kernel Function

- Use **quantum circuits to compute similarities** between data points in high-dimensional spaces.

Step 3: Train the Quantum SVM

- Use **classical SVM algorithms** (e.g., SciKit-Learn's SVM) with **Quantum Kernel Estimation.**

Step 4: Perform Classification

- Use quantum-enhanced hyperplane separation to classify unseen data points.

Hybrid Quantum-Classical AI Models

Hybrid Quantum-Classical AI models **combine classical machine learning techniques with quantum computing power.** Since **current quantum hardware is still developing,** hybrid models allow **seamless integration of quantum capabilities into existing AI workflows.**

1. How Hybrid Quantum-Classical Models Work

Stage	Classical Component	Quantum Component

Data Preprocessing	Feature scaling, data cleaning	Quantum feature encoding
Model Training	Uses classical optimizers (SGD, Adam)	Quantum Variational Circuits (VQCs) for weight updates
Inference & Prediction	Classical classification techniques	Quantum-enhanced decision-making

By combining **classical deep learning models with quantum neural networks (QNNs)**, hybrid models provide **scalability while benefiting from quantum parallelism**.

Code Example: Python Implementation of a Quantum Classifier

Let's implement a **Quantum Support Vector Machine (QSVM)** using **Qiskit Machine Learning**.

Step 1: Install Qiskit Machine Learning

Ensure you have **Qiskit's machine learning module** installed:

bash
CopyEdit
```
pip install qiskit-machine-learning
```

Step 2: Import Required Libraries

python
138

```
import numpy as np
from qiskit import QuantumCircuit, Aer
from qiskit.utils import algorithm_globals
from qiskit.circuit.library import ZZFeatureMap
from qiskit_machine_learning.kernels import QuantumKernel
from sklearn.svm import SVC
from sklearn.datasets import make_moons
from sklearn.model_selection import train_test_split
from sklearn.preprocessing import StandardScaler
```

Step 3: Generate and Preprocess Data

python

```
# Generate a synthetic dataset (two-class classification)
X, y = make_moons(n_samples=200, noise=0.15, random_state=42)

# Split into training and test sets
X_train, X_test, y_train, y_test = train_test_split(X, y,
test_size=0.2, random_state=42)

# Scale features
scaler = StandardScaler()
X_train = scaler.fit_transform(X_train)
X_test = scaler.transform(X_test)
```

Step 4: Define a Quantum Kernel Feature Map

python

```
# Create a 2-qubit quantum feature map
feature_map = ZZFeatureMap(feature_dimension=2, reps=2,
entanglement='linear')

# Define the quantum kernel
quantum_kernel = QuantumKernel(feature_map=feature_map,
quantum_instance=Aer.get_backend('qasm_simulator'))
```

Step 5: Train the Quantum SVM Classifier

python
CopyEdit
```python
# Train a classical SVM using the quantum kernel
svm = SVC(kernel=quantum_kernel.evaluate)
svm.fit(X_train, y_train)

# Predict on test set
y_pred = svm.predict(X_test)
```

Step 6: Evaluate the Quantum Classifier

python
CopyEdit
```python
from sklearn.metrics import accuracy_score

# Compute accuracy
accuracy = accuracy_score(y_test, y_pred)
print(f"Quantum SVM Accuracy: {accuracy:.2f}")
```

Step 7: Visualize Decision Boundaries

python
CopyEdit
```python
import matplotlib.pyplot as plt
import seaborn as sns

# Plot decision boundary
xx, yy = np.meshgrid(np.linspace(-2, 2, 100), np.linspace(-2, 2, 100))
```

```
Z = svm.predict(scaler.transform(np.c_[xx.ravel(),
yy.ravel()])).reshape(xx.shape)

plt.figure(figsize=(8,6))
sns.scatterplot(x=X_test[:, 0], y=X_test[:, 1], hue=y_test,
palette='coolwarm', edgecolor='black')
plt.contourf(xx, yy, Z, alpha=0.3, cmap='coolwarm')
plt.title("Quantum SVM Decision Boundary")
plt.show()
```

Building a **Quantum Classifier using QSVM** demonstrates the power of **Quantum Machine Learning (QML)** in **solving classification problems with improved efficiency**.

Quantum Kernel Methods enhance feature transformations in AI models.
QSVMs outperform classical SVMs in high-dimensional classification tasks.
Hybrid Quantum-Classical AI models combine classical deep learning with quantum acceleration.

As quantum hardware advances, **Quantum SVMs will become an essential tool in AI applications**, including **finance, healthcare, and cybersecurity**.

The next chapter will explore **Advanced Quantum Deep Learning Architectures** and how **Quantum Convolutional Neural Networks (QCNNs) are revolutionizing AI applications**.

Chapter 12

Quantum Generative Adversarial Networks (Quantum GANs)

Quantum Generative Adversarial Networks (**Quantum GANs**) represent a **fusion of quantum computing and deep learning**, offering **exponential speedup and enhanced learning capabilities** over classical GANs. They hold promise for **data generation, cryptography, drug discovery, and financial modeling**.

This chapter covers:

Introduction to Generative Adversarial Networks (GANs)
 How Quantum GANs Work
 Quantum Circuit Design for Generative AI

Introduction to Generative Adversarial Networks (GANs)

1. What Are GANs?

A **Generative Adversarial Network (GAN)** is a **deep learning model** used to generate **new, synthetic data** that resembles real-world examples. GANs are widely used in:

- **Image generation** (e.g., creating realistic deepfake images).
- **Data augmentation** (e.g., generating synthetic training data).
- **Drug discovery** (e.g., creating molecular structures).
- **Financial modeling** (e.g., generating synthetic stock market data).

GANs consist of **two neural networks—a Generator** and a **Discriminator**—which compete against each other.

GAN Architecture

plaintext

```
Real Data → Discriminator → Real or Fake?
                ↑
           Fake Data
                ↑
         Generator
```

- **Generator (G):** Creates synthetic data samples.
- **Discriminator (D):** Differentiates real data from generated (fake) data.
- **Training Goal:** The Generator improves until the Discriminator **cannot distinguish real from fake data**.

---

2. Classical GAN Training Workflow

1. The **Generator (G)** creates a **fake sample** from random noise.
2. The **Discriminator (D)** evaluates whether the sample is **real or fake**.
3. The **Discriminator updates** its weights to **improve classification accuracy**.
4. The **Generator updates** to **fool the Discriminator** better.
5. This process **continues until the Generator produces highly realistic samples**.

GANs are powerful but suffer from:

 Mode Collapse (Generator fails to create diverse samples).
  Training Instability (Difficult to optimize Generator and Discriminator simultaneously).
  High Computational Cost (GANs require massive GPUs for effective training).

Quantum computing offers solutions to these **challenges** through **Quantum GANs (QGANs)**.

How Quantum GANs Work

1. What is a Quantum GAN (QGAN)?

A **Quantum GAN (QGAN)** replaces classical neural networks with **quantum circuits**, allowing for:

Faster convergence using quantum parallelism.
Better data encoding using quantum states.
More complex probability distributions using **quantum entanglement**.

Key Difference: Instead of using **deep neural networks**, QGANs leverage **Quantum Variational Circuits (QVCs)** to **learn and generate complex patterns**.

---

2. Quantum GAN Architecture

Quantum GANs follow the same structure as classical GANs, with the Generator and Discriminator operating as **quantum circuits**.

```plaintext
CopyEdit
Quantum Noise → Quantum Generator → Quantum Discriminator →
Real or Fake?
                         ↑
          Quantum Variational Circuit
```

Quantum Components in QGANs

Component	Classical GAN	Quantum GAN (QGAN)
Generator (G)	Deep neural network (DNN)	**Quantum Variational Circuit (QVC)**
Discriminator (D)	Deep neural network (DNN)	**Hybrid Quantum-Classical Model**
Data Representation	Encodes data using classical vectors	Encodes data using **quantum states**

Training Speed	Slow on large datasets	**Exponential speedup** with quantum parallelism

Quantum GANs **outperform classical GANs in generating high-dimensional probability distributions**.

---

3. Training Process of Quantum GANs

The **Quantum GAN training process** follows the same adversarial principle as classical GANs but leverages **quantum properties**.

Step 1: Initialize Quantum Noise

- Instead of random classical vectors, QGANs **use quantum states** as noise input:

$|\psi\rangle = H|0\rangle$ | \psi \rangle = H | 0 \rangle $|\psi\rangle = H|0\rangle$

Step 2: Quantum Generator Creates Synthetic Data

- The **Quantum Generator** transforms quantum states into **feature representations** using **quantum gates**.
- Quantum feature maps encode the **latent space** into qubits.

Step 3: Quantum Discriminator Evaluates the Data

- The **Quantum Discriminator** uses **quantum measurement** to classify samples as **real or fake**.
- Hybrid QGANs often combine **quantum circuits with classical optimizers**.

Step 4: Update Quantum Circuit Parameters

- Quantum variational parameters are **optimized using gradient descent** and **quantum backpropagation**.

Step 5: Repeat Until the Generator Fools the Discriminator

- The **training loop continues** until the Discriminator cannot distinguish **real data from quantum-generated data.**

---

4. Quantum Circuit Design for Generative AI

A **Quantum Variational Circuit (QVC)** is used in **Quantum GAN Generators** to create **complex feature distributions**.

Example Quantum Generator Circuit (Qiskit Implementation)

python
CopyEdit
```
import numpy as np
from qiskit import QuantumCircuit, Aer, transpile, assemble,
execute
from qiskit.circuit import Parameter

# Define a quantum generator circuit with trainable parameters
num_qubits = 2
theta = Parameter('θ')

qc = QuantumCircuit(num_qubits)
qc.h(0)
qc.rx(theta, 1)
qc.cx(0, 1)
qc.measure_all()

qc.draw()
```

This quantum circuit:
  Uses a Hadamard gate (H) to create quantum superposition.
  Applies rotation gates (RX) to introduce trainable parameters.
  Uses a CNOT gate to create quantum entanglement.
  Performs quantum measurement for data sampling.

5. Applications of Quantum GANs

Quantum GANs are being explored in multiple **real-world applications**.

Industry	Application of QGANs
Finance	Generate synthetic stock market data
Cybersecurity	Improve anomaly detection & quantum encryption
Medical Research	Generate synthetic medical images & drug discovery
Quantum Chemistry	Model quantum molecular structures

Quantum GANs **outperform classical GANs** in generating **complex, high-dimensional data**.

Quantum Generative Adversarial Networks (**QGANs**) are a **breakthrough technology** that enhances **data generation using quantum mechanics**.

QGANs use Quantum Variational Circuits for improved generative modeling. Quantum GANs reduce computational overhead and accelerate training. QGANs have real-world applications in finance, healthcare, and cryptography.

As quantum hardware advances, **Quantum GANs will redefine AI-driven generative modeling**, making it possible to **generate complex, high-dimensional data faster than classical GANs**.

Applications in Quantum Image Generation and Data Augmentation

Quantum Generative Adversarial Networks (**QGANs**) have significant potential in **image generation and data augmentation**, allowing quantum-enhanced AI models to **generate realistic synthetic images and improve training datasets**.

1. Quantum Image Generation

Quantum GANs can **generate high-quality images** using quantum-enhanced feature mapping. Unlike classical deep learning, which **requires large-scale convolutional networks**, QGANs **encode pixel information into quantum states**, reducing the memory and processing requirements.

Advantages of Quantum Image Generation

Efficient Feature Encoding – Uses **quantum superposition** to represent complex patterns.
Enhanced Image Quality – Generates **high-dimensional features more efficiently**.
Improved Learning Capacity – Captures **intricate textures and patterns** using **quantum entanglement**.

Use Cases

Industry	Application of QGANs in Image Generation
Medical Imaging	Generate synthetic MRI and X-ray images for training AI models.
Autonomous Vehicles	Create realistic road scene simulations for AI training.
Creative Design	Generate AI-assisted artwork and deepfake images.

2. Data Augmentation with Quantum GANs

Data augmentation is **a critical technique** in AI training, helping models generalize better by **expanding the dataset size**. Quantum GANs can **generate realistic** variations of existing data, improving AI model performance in **low-data scenarios**.

How QGANs Improve Data Augmentation

Faster Synthetic Data Generation – QGANs **generate realistic variations of training samples**.

Improved Generalization – AI models trained with **QGAN-augmented data** achieve **higher accuracy**.

Reduces Bias in Training Data – Generates **diverse samples**, reducing overfitting.

Use Cases of Quantum Data Augmentation

Field	Application
Healthcare	Augment training data for disease detection models.
Cybersecurity	Generate synthetic attack patterns for training AI-based threat detection.
Natural Language Processing	Generate new text samples for AI language models.

Code Example: Implementing a Quantum GAN Using Qiskit

Now, let's implement a **basic Quantum GAN (QGAN) using Qiskit**. This will involve:

1. **Defining a Quantum Generator Circuit**
2. **Creating a Quantum Discriminator**
3. **Training the Quantum GAN**
4. **Evaluating the Generated Samples**

Step 1: Install Qiskit Machine Learning (If Not Installed)

Ensure that **Qiskit Machine Learning** is installed:

bash
CopyEdit
```bash
pip install qiskit qiskit-machine-learning
```

Step 2: Import Required Libraries

python
CopyEdit
```python
import numpy as np
import matplotlib.pyplot as plt
from qiskit import QuantumCircuit, Aer, transpile, assemble,
execute
from qiskit.circuit import Parameter
from qiskit.utils import algorithm_globals
from qiskit_machine_learning.algorithms import QGAN
from qiskit_machine_learning.datasets import gaussian

# Set random seed for reproducibility
algorithm_globals.random_seed = 42
```

Step 3: Define the Quantum Generator

python
CopyEdit
```python
def create_quantum_generator(num_qubits):
    theta = Parameter("θ")

    # Create a quantum circuit for the generator
    qc = QuantumCircuit(num_qubits)
```

```
# Apply a Hadamard gate to create a superposition
qc.h(range(num_qubits))

# Apply parameterized rotations
for i in range(num_qubits):
    qc.rx(theta, i)

# Entangle the qubits
qc.cx(0, 1)

return qc
```

This quantum circuit serves as the **Quantum Generator**, using **trainable parameters** to adjust **generated data distributions**.

Step 4: Define the Quantum Discriminator

python
CopyEdit

```
def quantum_discriminator(x):
    return np.tanh(2 * x)  # Classical activation function for
discrimination
```

Unlike classical GANs that use deep neural networks, this **Quantum Discriminator** uses a **simple non-linear function** to classify data.

Step 5: Load a Sample Dataset for Training

python
CopyEdit

```
# Generate synthetic training data
real_samples, _ = gaussian(num_samples=1000, num_features=1,
centers=2)
```

We use a **Gaussian distribution** as our training data, allowing the **Quantum Generator** to learn and generate similar distributions.

Step 6: Train the Quantum GAN

python
CopyEdit

```
# Define QGAN model
qgan = QGAN(
    real_samples,  # Real data
    num_qubits=2,  # Quantum Generator size
    generator_circuit=create_quantum_generator(2),  # Quantum
Generator
    discriminator=quantum_discriminator,  # Quantum
Discriminator
    tol_rel_ent_loss=0.01,  # Convergence threshold
    shots=1000,  # Number of quantum circuit runs
)

# Train QGAN model
qgan.train()
```

This step **trains the Quantum GAN** by optimizing the **Quantum Generator and Discriminator**.

Step 7: Evaluate the Generated Data

```python
CopyEdit
# Generate synthetic samples using the trained Quantum
Generator
synthetic_samples = qgan.generate(num_samples=100)

# Plot real vs. generated samples
plt.hist(real_samples, bins=30, alpha=0.5, label="Real Data")
plt.hist(synthetic_samples, bins=30, alpha=0.5,
label="Generated Data")
plt.legend()
plt.title("Comparison of Real vs. Generated Data")
plt.show()
```

If training is successful, the Quantum GAN will **generate samples that match the distribution of real data**.

Step 8: Deploy the QGAN on a Quantum Simulator

```python
CopyEdit
backend = Aer.get_backend("qasm_simulator")

# Execute the trained generator circuit
qobj = assemble(transpile(qgan.generator, backend))
result = backend.run(qobj).result()

# Print the generated quantum measurement results
print(result.get_counts())
```

This step **runs the Quantum Generator on IBM's quantum simulator**, ensuring that it functions correctly.

Key Insights from Our Quantum GAN Implementation

Quantum GANs replace classical deep learning with quantum circuits for enhanced generative modeling.
Quantum Data Augmentation improves AI model accuracy by generating diverse datasets.
Quantum Generative Models have real-world applications in finance, healthcare, and cybersecurity.

Quantum Generative Adversarial Networks (QGANs) offer breakthroughs in AI-generated data and synthetic image modeling.

QGANs generate high-dimensional feature spaces using quantum entanglement.
Quantum GANs reduce computational costs for generative modeling.
Real-world applications include finance, security, and medical research.

As quantum computing matures, Quantum GANs will redefine AI-based data generation, improving how AI models learn from synthetic datasets.

The next section will explore Building Advanced Quantum GANs for High-Resolution Image Generation.

Chapter 13

Practical Applications of Quantum Machine Learning

Quantum Machine Learning (QML) is rapidly evolving, and its applications are transforming multiple industries. Among the most impactful fields benefiting from QML are **drug discovery, healthcare, and financial modeling**. Traditional machine learning models, while powerful, often face computational bottlenecks when dealing with **complex molecular simulations, large-scale risk assessments, and high-dimensional data processing**.

Quantum AI provides a **paradigm shift** by leveraging quantum superposition, entanglement, and parallelism to tackle problems that classical AI struggles with. This chapter explores **Quantum AI's role in drug discovery, healthcare, and financial modeling**, demonstrating its real-world impact.

The Role of Quantum AI in Drug Discovery and Healthcare

1. Challenges in Classical Drug Discovery

Drug discovery is an **expensive and time-consuming** process. The current pharmaceutical industry spends billions of dollars in research and development, often requiring **over a decade** to bring a single drug to market. The key challenges include:

Challenge	Impact
High Computational Complexity	Simulating molecular interactions requires **massive computing power**.

Time-Consuming Drug Trials	Traditional methods take **years to analyze** molecular binding properties.
Inaccurate Drug Target Identification	Classical AI models struggle to **predict drug efficacy** accurately.
Costly Laboratory Experiments	Drug testing requires **significant financial investment**.

Quantum AI presents **a game-changing approach** to solving these problems by **accelerating molecular simulations, improving protein-ligand binding predictions, and optimizing drug formulations**.

---

2. How Quantum Machine Learning Enhances Drug Discovery

Quantum Machine Learning significantly improves the **speed and accuracy** of drug discovery through:

(a) Quantum-enhanced Molecular Simulations

- **Problem:** Classical computers struggle to accurately **simulate quantum interactions** within molecules.
- **Quantum AI Solution:** Quantum computing **naturally represents molecular interactions**, allowing for more **precise and efficient simulations** of drug-target interactions.

(b) Quantum Feature Mapping for Drug Discovery

- **Problem:** Identifying potential drug candidates requires analyzing **high-dimensional molecular features**.
- **Quantum AI Solution:** Quantum feature mapping enables **better pattern recognition**, improving drug screening.

(c) Quantum Variational Algorithms for Protein Folding

- **Problem:** Misfolded proteins are linked to diseases like **Alzheimer's and Parkinson's**. Classical AI requires **huge computational resources** to model protein folding.
- **Quantum AI Solution:** Quantum variational algorithms predict **stable protein structures faster**, enabling **breakthroughs in personalized medicine**.

(d) Quantum-assisted Genomic Data Processing

- **Problem: Genomic sequencing** generates petabytes of data, making classical processing slow and expensive.
- **Quantum AI Solution:** Quantum computing processes genomic data exponentially faster, identifying **genetic markers for diseases**.

---

3. Real-World Applications of Quantum AI in Healthcare

Application	How Quantum AI Improves It
Drug Discovery	Simulates molecular interactions **more efficiently**.
Personalized Medicine	Identifies **genetic variations** for better treatment.
Protein Folding Predictions	Solves complex **biological structure modeling**.
Medical Imaging	Improves **MRI and X-ray image processing** with

	quantum-enhanced deep learning.
Cancer Research	Detects **cancer cells faster** using quantum-enhanced image analysis.

With quantum AI, the **future of medicine is shifting towards precision treatments, accelerated drug development, and cost-efficient healthcare solutions**.

Financial Modeling and Quantum Risk Assessment

1. Limitations of Classical Financial AI

Financial markets are **inherently complex**, governed by **stochastic models, nonlinear patterns, and high-dimensional datasets**. Traditional AI models face limitations in:

Challenge	Impact
High Market Volatility	Classical models struggle to predict **unforeseen market crashes**.
Risk Analysis Complexity	Analyzing **high-dimensional risk factors** is computationally expensive.
Inefficient Portfolio Optimization	Classical AI lacks **real-time adaptability** to

	changing market conditions.
Algorithmic Trading Bottlenecks	Traditional models have **latency issues** in high-frequency trading.

Quantum AI solves these challenges by **introducing faster algorithms, better probabilistic modeling, and real-time market adaptation**.

---

2. How Quantum AI Enhances Financial Modeling

(a) Quantum Monte Carlo for Risk Simulation

- **Problem:** Classical Monte Carlo simulations require **billions of calculations** to assess financial risk.
- **Quantum AI Solution:** Quantum Monte Carlo speeds up simulations, allowing **faster and more accurate risk assessment**.

(b) Quantum Portfolio Optimization

- **Problem:** Selecting the optimal investment portfolio from **millions of assets** is computationally intense.
- **Quantum AI Solution:** Quantum computing evaluates **multiple asset combinations simultaneously**, optimizing **risk-return ratios instantly**.

(c) Quantum Variational Circuits for Fraud Detection

- **Problem:** Classical fraud detection models **fail to recognize sophisticated cyber-attacks**.
- **Quantum AI Solution:** Quantum-enhanced anomaly detection **identifies fraudulent transactions faster and more accurately**.

(d) Quantum Cryptography for Secure Financial Transactions

- **Problem: Cybersecurity threats in financial systems** are increasing.
- **Quantum AI Solution:** Quantum cryptography ensures **unbreakable security** in financial transactions.

3. Real-World Applications of Quantum AI in Finance

Financial Domain	How Quantum AI is Transforming It
Stock Market Prediction	Quantum AI improves accuracy in **stock price forecasting**.
Algorithmic Trading	Enables **faster high-frequency trading** strategies.
Risk Management	Enhances **financial risk analysis and fraud detection**.
Blockchain Security	Quantum cryptography ensures **tamper-proof financial transactions**.
Investment Banking	Optimizes **complex portfolio allocations** in real-time.

With **Quantum AI**, financial institutions **can process complex market data faster, reduce risk, and improve decision-making in real-time**.

Quantum AI is **revolutionizing both healthcare and financial industries**, bringing unprecedented advancements in **drug discovery, medical research, financial risk analysis, and trading**.

 Quantum AI accelerates drug discovery through molecular simulations and protein folding analysis.
 Quantum Machine Learning enhances financial modeling, risk assessment, and fraud detection.

160

Quantum computing ensures high-speed optimization and better decision-making in complex domains.

As **quantum technology evolves**, these applications will become mainstream, **transforming how industries operate and unlocking new frontiers in AI-driven problem-solving**.

The Impact of Quantum AI on Cybersecurity and Cryptography

Cybersecurity and cryptography are at the heart of **digital security**, protecting sensitive information in **financial transactions, national security, personal privacy, and enterprise data management**. However, the **rise of quantum computing** introduces both **threats and opportunities** to cybersecurity.

- **Threat:** Classical encryption methods (RSA, ECC, AES) may become **obsolete** due to quantum algorithms capable of breaking them.
- **Opportunity:** Quantum cryptography and Quantum AI introduce **new secure cryptographic frameworks** resistant to quantum attacks.

This section explores the **impact of Quantum AI on cybersecurity and cryptography**, demonstrating **how quantum computing enhances security while posing challenges to traditional encryption**.

---

1. Why Classical Cybersecurity is at Risk?

(a) Vulnerability of Classical Encryption to Quantum Attacks

Most of today's cybersecurity systems rely on **public-key encryption**, which is based on the difficulty of solving **mathematical problems like integer factorization and discrete logarithms**.

Encryption Method	Security Basis	Quantum Threat

RSA (Rivest-Shamir-Adleman)	Integer Factorization	**Shor's Algorithm** can factorize numbers exponentially faster.
ECC (Elliptic Curve Cryptography)	Discrete Logarithms	Vulnerable to **quantum attacks** on elliptic curves.
AES (Advanced Encryption Standard)	Symmetric Encryption	**Grover's Algorithm** speeds up brute-force attacks.

If a **large-scale quantum computer** is built, it could **decrypt secure communications, financial transactions, and classified information in seconds**.

---

2. How Quantum AI Improves Cybersecurity

(a) Post-Quantum Cryptography (PQC)

Since classical encryption is at risk, **Post-Quantum Cryptography (PQC)** is being developed to create **quantum-resistant security algorithms**. These methods use **lattice-based cryptography, hash-based signatures, and multivariate equations**.

Quantum-Resistant Algorithm	Security Basis
Lattice-based Cryptography	Hard mathematical problems resistant to quantum computing.
Code-based Cryptography	Uses error-correcting codes instead of factorization.
Hash-based Cryptography	Secure against quantum computing due to its one-way function properties.

Quantum AI helps **optimize these cryptographic schemes**, ensuring **secure post-quantum encryption**.

(b) Quantum Key Distribution (QKD)

Quantum Key Distribution (QKD) uses the **principles of quantum mechanics** to create **unbreakable encryption keys**.

- **How it works:**

    - Secure quantum keys are exchanged using **entangled photon pairs**.
    - If an eavesdropper intercepts the key, **quantum states collapse**, revealing the attack.
- **Use Cases:**
  Government and military communications
  Financial transactions in banking
  Secure cloud computing

One of the most well-known QKD protocols is the **BB84 protocol**, which guarantees **tamper-proof encryption**.

(c) Quantum AI for Intrusion Detection and Threat Prediction

Cybersecurity systems require **fast threat detection** and **anomaly recognition**. Quantum AI **enhances threat detection models

Chapter 14

Challenges and Limitations of Quantum Machine Learning (QML)

Quantum Machine Learning (QML) is a groundbreaking field that combines quantum computing with artificial intelligence to solve complex problems **faster and more efficiently** than classical computing. However, despite its promise, QML **faces major challenges** that limit its practical implementation today.

Among the most significant obstacles are **hardware limitations and the issue of noisy quantum systems**. These factors impact the scalability, accuracy, and reliability of quantum AI applications. In this chapter, we explore these limitations in detail, providing insights into the **current state of quantum hardware, noise issues, and the road ahead** for Quantum AI.

Hardware Limitations in Quantum AI Systems

1. Current State of Quantum Hardware

Unlike classical computing, where processors have evolved through Moore's Law (doubling transistors every two years), **quantum computing is still in its infancy**. Today's quantum processors are far from achieving the scale required for **large-scale AI applications**.

Key Limitations of Existing Quantum Hardware

Limitation	Impact on Quantum AI
Qubit Stability	Quantum bits (qubits) are highly fragile and lose information quickly.

Scalability Issues	Current quantum computers have **limited qubit counts**, restricting complex AI applications.
Quantum Decoherence	Qubits interact with the environment, leading to **loss of quantum information**.
Quantum Gate Errors	Quantum operations are error-prone, leading to incorrect AI model training.
High Operational Costs	Maintaining a quantum system requires **extreme cooling (near absolute zero)** and complex infrastructure.

The **performance of quantum AI models heavily depends on the quality and number of available qubits**. Current quantum processors are still in the range of **tens to hundreds of qubits**, whereas practical quantum AI requires thousands to millions of error-corrected qubits.

---

2. Qubit Stability and Error Rates

(a) The Challenge of Maintaining Qubit Coherence

A qubit's ability to **retain its state** is called **coherence time**. Quantum AI models need **long coherence times** to perform deep learning tasks, but existing hardware has **short-lived qubits**.

Quantum Hardware	Coherence Time
Superconducting Qubits (IBM, Google)	50–100 microseconds

Trapped Ions (IonQ, Honeywell)	~10 milliseconds
Photonic Qubits (Xanadu, PsiQuantum)	Much longer but difficult to scale

The shorter the coherence time, the harder it is to run complex AI models.

(b) Quantum Gate Errors and Fault Tolerance

Quantum computers rely on **quantum gates** to manipulate qubits, similar to how classical computers use logic gates. However, quantum gates have **high error rates**, reducing the accuracy of QML models.

Common Quantum Errors:

1. **Bit Flip Error:** A qubit flips from **0 to 1** due to environmental interference.
2. **Phase Flip Error:** A qubit's phase is altered, leading to incorrect computations.
3. **Depolarization:** Qubit state is lost due to external noise.

Without **error correction**, quantum AI models produce **inaccurate results**, limiting their real-world applications.

---

3. Scalability Challenges in Quantum AI

For Quantum AI to surpass classical AI, it needs **scalable quantum hardware** with error correction. The challenge is **building large-scale fault-tolerant quantum computers**.

- **IBM's Quantum Roadmap** targets a **100,000+ qubit machine** by 2033.
- **Google's Quantum AI team** is working on **quantum error correction breakthroughs**.
- **PsiQuantum** is developing a **million-qubit photonic quantum processor** for AI.

Current quantum hardware **cannot yet support large-scale AI models** like GPT-4 or AlphaFold due to these hardware limitations.

The Issue of Noisy Quantum Systems

1. What is Quantum Noise?

Quantum computers **do not operate in isolation**—they interact with their surroundings, leading to **quantum noise**. Noise causes **qubit errors, decoherence, and inaccurate results** in Quantum AI models.

Types of Quantum Noise

Noise Type	Effect on Quantum AI
Decoherence Noise	Qubits lose quantum states due to environmental interference.
Gate Noise	Errors occur when quantum gates are applied.
Measurement Noise	Readout errors in qubit measurement impact AI predictions.
Cross-Talk Noise	One qubit's state affects another, disrupting calculations.

Quantum noise **limits the depth of quantum circuits**, making it difficult to train complex AI models.

---

2. The Impact of Noise on Quantum AI

Quantum AI models **require precise qubit manipulations**, but noise introduces **uncertainty and incorrect outputs**.

(a) Reduced Model Accuracy

- Noisy qubits **introduce errors in Quantum Neural Networks (QNNs)**.
- **Quantum Generative Models (Quantum GANs)** fail to generate realistic data.

167

(b) Limited Circuit Depth

- Quantum circuits cannot perform **deep computations** due to **rapid decoherence**.
- AI models need **many iterations**, but noise restricts processing power.

(c) Unreliable Training Process

- Quantum Variational Circuits (**used in Quantum ML models**) **drift over time**, causing **unstable AI training**.
- **Quantum-enhanced reinforcement learning** suffers from noise, reducing decision-making accuracy.

Noisy Quantum AI models are far from achieving real-world deployment.

3. Methods to Reduce Noise in Quantum AI

Researchers are developing techniques to **reduce quantum noise** and improve the reliability of QML models.

(a) Quantum Error Correction (QEC)

Quantum Error Correction (QEC) uses **multiple qubits to encode information redundantly**, protecting it from noise.

Error Correction Method	How It Helps
Surface Codes	Stores one logical qubit across multiple physical qubits.
Quantum Repetition Codes	Detects and corrects bit-flip errors.
Topological Qubits	More stable qubits with built-in noise resistance.

Major players like **IBM, Google, and Microsoft** are investing heavily in **error-corrected quantum computing**.

(b) Noisy Intermediate-Scale Quantum (NISQ) Era Solutions

Since large-scale **fault-tolerant quantum computers** are still a decade away, researchers are exploring **Noisy Intermediate-Scale Quantum (NISQ) methods**.

NISQ Solution	Purpose
Quantum Machine Learning Hybrid Models	Combine quantum AI with classical deep learning.
Noise Mitigation Algorithms	Reduce quantum noise post-processing.
Quantum Circuit Optimization	Reduces quantum gate operations to lower errors.

Even though **NISQ devices** are noisy, they still **demonstrate Quantum AI advantages** in small-scale problems.

Future Outlook for Quantum AI

Despite hardware limitations and noise challenges, Quantum AI is progressing rapidly.

IBM and Google are leading in **quantum error correction research**.
Hybrid Quantum-Classical AI models are being explored to **bridge the gap**.
Quantum hardware startups (IonQ, Rigetti, Xanadu) are developing **scalable quantum processors**.

Overcoming these challenges will enable Quantum AI to revolutionize industries **from healthcare to finance to cybersecurity**.

Quantum AI has **extraordinary potential**, but it is **currently limited by hardware constraints and quantum noise**.

Qubit instability, gate errors, and decoherence reduce Quantum AI efficiency. Quantum noise makes training AI models on quantum computers unreliable. Quantum Error Correction and Hybrid AI models offer short-term solutions.

As **quantum hardware improves**, these challenges **will be overcome**, unlocking **the true power of Quantum AI**.

The next section will explore **Ethical Considerations and Future Directions of Quantum AI**, including **privacy, security, and the societal impact of quantum intelligence**.

Quantum Error Correction Techniques

Quantum Error Correction (QEC) is a fundamental component of **fault-tolerant quantum computing**. Unlike classical systems where errors can be detected and corrected using redundancy (e.g., error-checking bits in digital communications), quantum computing faces unique challenges due to **quantum decoherence, measurement errors, and gate noise**.

To make **Quantum Machine Learning (QML) practical**, robust error correction methods are essential to maintain **the integrity of quantum computations** over long periods. This section explores **leading QEC techniques, their principles, and applications in Quantum AI**.

1. Why is Quantum Error Correction (QEC) Needed?

Quantum systems are **extremely fragile**. Qubits lose information due to **decoherence** (interaction with the environment) and **quantum gate errors** (imperfect operations). These errors **accumulate over time**, making it difficult for Quantum AI models to maintain **reliable calculations**.

Key error sources in Quantum AI include:

Error Type	Cause	Impact on QML

Bit Flip Error	Random qubit flips from **	0⟩ to
Phase Flip Error	Qubit's **phase changes** unexpectedly	Loss of information in quantum neural networks
Depolariza tion	Qubit loses **all quantum information**	Model becomes **unusable** for AI training
Readout Noise	Measurement errors distort results	**Unreliable AI predictions**

To **make Quantum AI scalable**, we need **error correction techniques** to **detect, prevent, and correct these quantum errors**.

2. Quantum Error Correction Techniques

Unlike classical error correction, **quantum errors cannot be copied (due to the No-Cloning Theorem)**. Instead, QEC **spreads quantum information across multiple qubits** to protect it. The most widely used quantum error correction methods are:

(a) Quantum Repetition Codes (Bit Flip & Phase Flip Correction)

This is the **simplest error correction method**, inspired by classical repetition codes.

- **How it works:**

  - Instead of using **one qubit**, the quantum state is **spread across multiple qubits**.
  - For example, encoding $|\psi\rangle$ as: $|\psi\rangle \rightarrow |\psi\psi\psi\rangle |\psi\rangle \rightarrow |\psi\psi\psi\rangle |\psi\rangle \rightarrow |\psi\psi\psi\rangle$
  - If an error occurs in one qubit, the other two can **help correct it**.
- **Limitations:**

  - Cannot correct **simultaneous bit and phase errors**.
  - Requires **many physical qubits per logical qubit**.

(b) Surface Code (Leading Fault-Tolerant QEC Technique)

The **Surface Code** is currently the most promising QEC technique for **large-scale quantum computers**.

- **How it works:**

    - Uses a **grid of qubits** where **some qubits store information**, and **others detect errors**.
    - Any errors can be **detected and corrected without measuring the logical qubits** directly.
- **Advantages:**
Works for **large-scale quantum computers**
Can correct **both bit and phase errors**
Used by **Google, IBM, and Microsoft** for error-resistant quantum computing

- **Challenges:**
Requires **thousands of physical qubits per logical qubit**
High overhead cost

(c) Quantum Low-Density Parity-Check (QLDPC) Codes

Quantum LDPC codes **extend classical LDPC error correction** to quantum systems. They offer **improved fault tolerance** with **fewer qubits required per logical qubit**.

- **Advantages:**
More efficient than **Surface Code**
Requires **fewer physical qubits**

- **Limitations:**
Still in **experimental research phase**
Implementation challenges with **current quantum hardware**

3. Fault-Tolerant Quantum AI: Overcoming Hardware Noise

Since **perfect quantum computers do not yet exist**, Quantum AI researchers **use hybrid error mitigation techniques** to handle errors **in real-time**.

(a) Quantum Error Mitigation (QEM)

- Unlike QEC, **QEM reduces errors without using extra qubits**.
- **Methods include:**
  Noise-aware quantum training
  Post-processing noise reduction
  Quantum circuit optimization

(b) Hybrid Quantum-Classical AI

- Many **Quantum AI applications** rely on **classical machine learning models** to **correct noisy quantum outputs**.
- This **bridges the gap** until fault-tolerant quantum systems become available.

Table: Comparison of Classical AI vs. Quantum AI - Limitations and Future Scope

Feature	Classical AI	Quantum AI
Processing Power	Limited by **classical CPU & GPU capabilities**	Uses **quantum parallelism** for speedup
Data Encoding	Stores data as **binary (0s and 1s)**	Stores data as **quantum states (superposition & entanglement)**
Error Handling	Classical error correction is **well-developed**	**Quantum noise and decoherence** remain a challenge
Scalability	Can handle **billions of parameters (Deep Learning)**	Requires **error-corrected qubits** for large-scale applications

AI Model Training	Takes days/weeks for complex AI models	Quantum AI could reduce training to **minutes/hours**
Current Hardware	**Mature** (GPUs, TPUs, supercomputers)	**Limited qubit count & noisy systems**
Security	**Vulnerable** to quantum attacks (RSA, ECC encryption)	**Quantum Cryptography** enhances security
Future Potential	AI improvements depend on **faster classical hardware**	**Scalability depends on quantum error correction breakthroughs**

Key Takeaways:

Classical AI is efficient today but has computational limits.
Quantum AI has the potential for exponential speedup, but hardware limitations slow adoption.
Fault-tolerant quantum computing will be the biggest breakthrough for scalable Quantum AI.

Quantum Machine Learning (QML) is transforming AI, but quantum errors and hardware limitations remain the biggest challenges.

Quantum Error Correction (QEC) is essential for large-scale Quantum AI applications.
Techniques like Surface Codes and Quantum Repetition Codes help reduce errors.
Hybrid Quantum-Classical AI models offer short-term solutions for real-world applications.

As Quantum Error Correction advances, Quantum AI will become mainstream, unlocking applications in drug discovery, finance, cybersecurity, and beyond.

Let us move on to Chapter 15: The Future of AI and Quantum Computing The Road to Quantum Advantage in AI

Chapter 15

The Future of AI and Quantum Computing

Artificial Intelligence (AI) has evolved rapidly over the past decade, transforming industries through machine learning, deep learning, and neural networks. However, as AI models become increasingly complex, they demand exponentially greater computational power, which classical hardware struggles to provide. Quantum computing, with its ability to process information in parallel and solve problems beyond the reach of classical systems, is emerging as a potential solution to these computational bottlenecks.

Quantum AI, the fusion of quantum computing and artificial intelligence, represents the next frontier in technological advancement. The transition from classical AI to Quantum AI is not immediate, but research and investments in quantum computing are accelerating. This chapter explores the path toward quantum advantage in AI, detailing the challenges, opportunities, and milestones that will define the future of AI and quantum computing.

The Road to Quantum Advantage in AI

Quantum advantage refers to the point at which a quantum computer can solve a problem faster or more efficiently than the most powerful classical supercomputers. While quantum supremacy, demonstrated by Google in 2019, proved that quantum processors could outperform classical ones on a specific computational task, quantum advantage extends this concept to practical, real-world applications, including AI and machine learning.

Achieving quantum advantage in AI requires breakthroughs in quantum hardware, algorithms, and software. Despite the challenges, the roadmap toward quantum AI is becoming increasingly clear, with key developments shaping its trajectory.

1. Advancements in Quantum Hardware

Quantum AI's potential is constrained by current quantum hardware limitations, particularly in terms of qubit stability, coherence time, and error rates. To reach quantum advantage, hardware improvements are necessary across multiple dimensions.

Increasing Qubit Count and Stability

Quantum AI applications require thousands to millions of high-fidelity qubits. Today's quantum computers operate with a limited number of qubits, most of which are prone to noise and decoherence. Companies like IBM, Google, IonQ, and Rigetti are working on scaling qubit counts while improving coherence times to enable deeper quantum circuits for AI applications.

Error Correction and Fault Tolerance

Quantum error correction is essential for large-scale AI models running on quantum hardware. Current quantum systems suffer from significant noise, making it difficult to execute complex AI algorithms reliably. Advances in fault-tolerant quantum computing, such as surface codes and logical qubits, will be crucial in mitigating these errors and stabilizing quantum AI models.

Quantum Processing Speed and Connectivity

Quantum speedup in AI depends on high-speed quantum gates and low-latency qubit interactions. Hardware innovations in superconducting qubits, trapped ions, photonic quantum computing, and topological qubits aim to enhance processing speeds, enabling faster and more scalable Quantum AI.

2. Development of Quantum AI Algorithms

Quantum AI will only achieve practical advantage when quantum algorithms surpass classical methods in efficiency, accuracy, and applicability. Researchers are actively developing new quantum machine learning techniques that leverage quantum parallelism and entanglement to accelerate AI training and inference.

Quantum Neural Networks (QNNs) and Quantum Deep Learning

Quantum neural networks represent a new class of AI models where quantum circuits replace classical neurons. By leveraging quantum states, QNNs can process information in fundamentally different ways, potentially leading to breakthroughs in pattern recognition, generative modeling, and reinforcement learning.

Quantum Feature Mapping and Data Encoding

A major challenge in Quantum AI is encoding classical data into quantum states efficiently. Quantum feature mapping techniques are being refined to enable seamless integration of classical datasets into quantum computing frameworks, improving classification, clustering, and optimization tasks.

Quantum Kernel Methods for Machine Learning

Quantum kernel estimation has shown promise in support vector machines and other AI applications. These quantum-enhanced algorithms allow AI models to work with higher-dimensional feature spaces, improving accuracy and computational efficiency in tasks like fraud detection, medical diagnosis, and natural language processing.

3. Hybrid Quantum-Classical AI Systems

Since fully error-corrected quantum computers are not yet available, the near-term approach to Quantum AI involves hybrid models that combine quantum and classical computing. Hybrid architectures allow AI models to leverage quantum speedup for specific subproblems while relying on classical hardware for other computations.

Quantum-Assisted AI Training

Quantum AI models can accelerate certain aspects of deep learning, such as weight optimization, feature selection, and hyperparameter tuning. By offloading computationally expensive components to quantum processors, AI training times can be significantly reduced.

Variational Quantum Algorithms in AI

Variational quantum algorithms (VQAs) are among the most promising techniques for near-term Quantum AI. These algorithms use quantum circuits to perform optimization tasks while classical computers adjust the quantum parameters. Applications include variational quantum classifiers, generative quantum models, and quantum-enhanced reinforcement learning.

4. Industry Adoption and Real-World Applications

The path to quantum advantage in AI is being paved by both academic research and corporate investments. Various industries are already experimenting with quantum computing for AI applications, demonstrating early signs of quantum advantage.

Healthcare and Drug Discovery

177

Quantum AI has the potential to revolutionize drug discovery by enabling more accurate molecular simulations, protein folding predictions, and genomics analysis. Pharmaceutical companies are collaborating with quantum computing firms to accelerate drug development and personalized medicine.

Financial Modeling and Risk Assessment

Quantum AI enhances risk modeling and financial predictions by processing high-dimensional datasets more efficiently than classical models. Quantum Monte Carlo simulations and quantum-enhanced portfolio optimization are among the key use cases.

Cybersecurity and Quantum Cryptography

Quantum AI plays a critical role in post-quantum cryptography and cybersecurity. As quantum computers threaten existing encryption standards, Quantum AI enables the development of quantum-resistant cryptographic protocols and secure AI-driven threat detection systems.

Supply Chain Optimization and Logistics

Quantum AI can optimize complex logistical problems by finding near-optimal solutions to supply chain networks, traffic routing, and resource allocation. Quantum-inspired AI models are already being tested to improve operational efficiency in global industries.

5. The Road Ahead for Quantum AI

The journey toward quantum advantage in AI will be shaped by several key milestones:

- **Short-Term (Next 5 Years)**

    - Expansion of hybrid quantum-classical AI models
    - Improved quantum error mitigation techniques
    - Commercial adoption of quantum-assisted AI in niche applications
- **Medium-Term (5–10 Years)**

    - Demonstration of quantum advantage in select AI problems
    - Advancements in fault-tolerant quantum computing
    - Increased availability of cloud-based quantum AI platforms
- **Long-Term (Beyond 10 Years)**

- Fully scalable quantum AI systems with millions of qubits
- Widespread adoption of quantum AI in healthcare, finance, and scientific research
- Emergence of artificial general intelligence (AGI) powered by quantum computing

The realization of quantum advantage in AI will require sustained research, technological breakthroughs, and industry collaboration. As quantum computing matures, AI models will evolve to leverage its full computational potential, unlocking new possibilities that are currently beyond the limits of classical AI.

Emerging Trends in Quantum AI Research

Quantum Artificial Intelligence (Quantum AI) is rapidly advancing as researchers explore new ways to leverage quantum computing for machine learning and artificial intelligence. The intersection of quantum computing and AI presents unique opportunities to solve problems that are computationally infeasible for classical systems. However, as the field evolves, new research directions are emerging that will define the next decade of Quantum AI development.

1. Quantum AI for High-Dimensional Optimization

Optimization problems are central to AI, spanning areas such as deep learning model training, reinforcement learning, and data clustering. Quantum computing is inherently suited for solving optimization problems faster than classical methods, and researchers are exploring how quantum-enhanced optimization techniques can be applied to AI.

Quantum Approximate Optimization Algorithm (QAOA)

QAOA is one of the most studied quantum algorithms for combinatorial optimization. It has been applied to AI tasks such as:

- Feature selection in machine learning models
- Hyperparameter tuning in deep learning
- Resource allocation and scheduling in AI-driven automation systems

Quantum-Inspired Metaheuristics

179

Quantum-inspired techniques, such as simulated quantum annealing and quantum-inspired neural networks, are being researched to improve optimization efficiency even on classical hardware.

---

2. Quantum AI for Natural Language Processing (NLP)

Quantum-enhanced NLP research is in its early stages, but it has the potential to revolutionize how AI processes language. Since NLP relies on processing vast amounts of data and complex linguistic patterns, quantum AI could offer significant improvements.

Quantum NLP and Sentence Encoding

Quantum NLP aims to leverage quantum states to represent words, phrases, and sentences in high-dimensional Hilbert space, allowing for more efficient semantic understanding. Potential applications include:

- Faster machine translation
- More accurate chatbots and AI assistants
- Improved search algorithms

Quantum Transformers for AI

Transformers, the foundation of modern NLP models like GPT and BERT, require large-scale matrix operations. Quantum versions of transformers could enable more efficient training and inference, reducing energy consumption and time required for AI-driven text processing.

---

3. Hybrid Quantum-Classical Deep Learning Models

Until fully scalable quantum computers become available, hybrid models that integrate quantum and classical computing will dominate Quantum AI research. These models seek to harness the advantages of quantum computing while leveraging classical AI frameworks.

Quantum-Assisted Neural Networks

Quantum-assisted AI models utilize quantum circuits to enhance deep learning models in areas such as:

- Quantum Variational Classifiers (QVC)
- Quantum-enhanced reinforcement learning for autonomous systems
- Quantum-assisted generative adversarial networks (GANs)

Quantum Feature Engineering

Quantum feature mapping is being actively researched to enhance classical machine learning models. By encoding features into quantum states, researchers aim to create better representations for AI models, improving classification accuracy in complex datasets.

---

4. Scalable Quantum AI Hardware and Cloud Computing

As Quantum AI evolves, cloud-based quantum computing services are becoming more accessible. Companies such as IBM, Google, Amazon, and Microsoft are offering quantum cloud platforms, enabling researchers and businesses to experiment with Quantum AI without requiring dedicated quantum hardware.

Quantum Cloud AI Services

- IBM Quantum Experience provides APIs for developing quantum-enhanced AI applications.
- Google Quantum AI Lab explores how quantum hardware can accelerate deep learning.
- Amazon Braket allows developers to experiment with quantum machine learning on different quantum hardware architectures.

Developing Scalable Quantum AI Processors

Research in hardware scalability focuses on:

- Increasing qubit counts for large-scale AI models
- Reducing quantum gate error rates

- Implementing fault-tolerant quantum circuits for AI applications

---

Preparing for a Quantum AI Future

Quantum AI is transitioning from theoretical research to practical applications. Organizations, governments, and technology leaders are actively preparing for the impact of quantum-enhanced AI systems.

1. Workforce Development and Quantum AI Education

As Quantum AI matures, there is an increasing demand for skilled professionals who can bridge the gap between quantum computing and artificial intelligence. Universities and online platforms are expanding their curricula to include:

- Courses in Quantum Machine Learning
- Training programs on Quantum Programming with Qiskit, Cirq, and PennyLane
- Interdisciplinary AI-Quantum computing research initiatives

Leading institutions, including MIT, Stanford, and Oxford, are developing Quantum AI research centers to train the next generation of scientists and engineers.

2. Quantum AI Adoption in Industries

Industries are exploring how Quantum AI can improve business processes, enhance decision-making, and optimize AI-driven operations.

Healthcare and Drug Discovery

Pharmaceutical companies are investing in Quantum AI for:

- Simulating complex molecular interactions
- Discovering new drugs and accelerating clinical trials
- Predicting protein structures more efficiently

Finance and Market Prediction

Financial institutions are exploring:

- Quantum-enhanced portfolio optimization
- Faster risk assessment models for global markets
- Fraud detection using quantum-enhanced anomaly detection

Cybersecurity and AI Threat Intelligence

Governments and enterprises are integrating Quantum AI for:

- Quantum-resistant encryption to protect against cyber threats
- AI-powered quantum threat detection systems
- Post-quantum security frameworks

3. Overcoming Quantum AI Challenges

Despite its potential, Quantum AI must overcome key challenges, including:

- **Scalability of quantum hardware** to support large-scale AI applications
- **Quantum noise and decoherence** that affect AI model accuracy
- **High costs of quantum computing infrastructure** limiting accessibility

Companies and research institutions are collaborating on solutions, including hybrid architectures and advanced error correction techniques, to enable reliable and practical Quantum AI.

Ethical Considerations and Security Risks in Quantum Machine Learning

Quantum AI introduces new ethical and security challenges that must be addressed as the technology evolves.

1. The Ethics of Quantum AI Decision-Making

As Quantum AI systems become more capable, ethical concerns surrounding bias, transparency, and fairness in AI models will become more significant. Quantum AI has the potential to amplify existing AI biases if not properly designed.

Quantum AI and Algorithmic Fairness

- Ensuring that quantum-enhanced AI models do not replicate or exacerbate biases present in classical datasets
- Developing fairness-aware quantum machine learning algorithms
- Addressing ethical concerns in AI decision-making for sensitive applications like criminal justice, healthcare, and hiring processes

Regulatory Considerations for Quantum AI

- Governments and policymakers must establish ethical guidelines for Quantum AI deployment.
- Research is needed to create standards for explainable Quantum AI models.
- International cooperation is essential to prevent misuse of Quantum AI for malicious purposes.

2. Security Risks of Quantum AI in Cybersecurity and Cryptography

Quantum computing poses both risks and solutions for cybersecurity. While it enables breakthroughs in AI-driven security, it also threatens current cryptographic protocols.

Post-Quantum Cryptography and Quantum Threats

- RSA and ECC encryption will become vulnerable once large-scale quantum computers are operational.
- Quantum AI could be used for adversarial attacks on classical AI models.
- Organizations must develop post-quantum cryptographic solutions to ensure future-proof security.

Quantum AI and Data Privacy

- Quantum AI's ability to process vast amounts of data raises concerns about user privacy.
- Ethical quantum AI frameworks should focus on securing sensitive data in AI-driven applications.
- Quantum homomorphic encryption is being researched to allow AI models to process encrypted data without compromising security.

3. The Need for Global Collaboration in Quantum AI Ethics

Quantum AI's implications extend beyond national borders. International cooperation is needed to ensure responsible development and deployment of Quantum AI systems.

Establishing Quantum AI Ethical Guidelines

- Governments, technology companies, and research institutions must work together to create ethical standards for Quantum AI.
- The development of ethical AI frameworks should consider the impact of quantum decision-making in various industries.

Preventing Quantum AI Misuse

- Quantum AI could be weaponized for cyber warfare and adversarial AI attacks.
- International treaties and agreements will be necessary to regulate Quantum AI development and usage.

Quantum AI presents a transformative leap in artificial intelligence, yet its ethical and security considerations must be addressed to ensure its responsible integration into society. As researchers, industry leaders, and policymakers collaborate to navigate the opportunities and risks, the future of Quantum AI will depend on how well these challenges are managed.